The Archaeology of Hill Farming on Exmoor

Edwin farmed in complete isolation at Lank Combe
(Lacoma in 1086), in the 'long valley' running westwards
up from Badgworthy Water, below Brendon Common,
with only the ravens and the eagles to keep him company.

(Hoskins 1954, 56)

The Archaeology of Hill Farming on Exmoor

by Cain Hegarty

with Rob Wilson-North

ENGLISH HERITAGE

EXMOOR
NATIONAL PARK
Celebrating 60 years
1954 – 2014

Published by English Heritage, The Engine House, Fire Fly Avenue, Swindon SN2 2EH
www.english-heritage.org.uk
English Heritage is the Government's lead body for the historic environment.

First published 2014

ISBN 978–1-84802–082–5

Product code 51600

British Library Cataloguing in Publication data
A CIP catalogue record for this book is available from the British Library.

For more information about English Heritage images, contact Archive Research
Services, The Engine House, Fire Fly Avenue, Swindon SN2 2EH;
telephone (01793) 414600.

Brought to publication by Sarah Enticknap, Publishing, English Heritage
Typeset in Charter Regular ITC 9.5pt
Edited by Jeremy Toynbee
Indexed by Osprey Indexing
Page layout by Pauline Hull Design
Printed in the UK by Park Communications Ltd

CONTENTS

ACKNOWLEDGEMENTS

This book derives from the information gathered in the National Mapping Programme Survey of Exmoor National Park. Throughout that endeavour there have been some key individuals at English Heritage and Exmoor National Park Authority without whom this book would not have become a reality: Helen Winton has given so freely of her time and knowledge in bringing this whole project to completion; Faye Glover and Jess Turner have patiently helped with endless enquiries and requests for information; Hazel Riley, Elaine Jamieson and the rest of the former English Heritage Exeter Survey Office team, whose experience and knowledge of south-west uplands has helped shape this book and some of whose field survey, since 2000, is represented in these pages; and Kathy Toms who worked on the mapping phase of the Exmoor National Mapping Programme project.

Other individuals have shared their knowledge of various aspects of Exmoor's historic landscape: Mary Siraut (County Editor of the Somerset Victoria County History) for very helpful discussion based on her detailed knowledge of the Exmoor sources and for reading some of the text; David Lloyd for discussion and the chance to draw on his encyclopedic knowledge of Exmoor's moorlands; Isabel Richardson and Shirley Blaylock for their expertise and knowledge of the Acland estates; Ralph Fyfe (University of Plymouth) for helpful comments and advice and an astonishing knowledge of Exmoor's blanket peat and valley mires; David James Ramsay for his freely shared research and information and his passion for the Brendon valley and beyond, and to all who contributed their knowledge about Exmoor's turf cutting, particularly Santa Lafuenti, Roy Kellaway and John Pile; Mr and Mrs Robinson of North Furzehill for their time and enthusiasm and for sharing their experiences of water power on Exmoor.

Others have given of their specialist knowledge from nearby and further afield: Jon Gregory and Tom Williamson (University of East Anglia); Dr Anne Marie Tindley at Glasgow Caledonian University; Daniel Bishop for sharing his knowledge of thatch and thatching; Jonathan Brown and Dr Roy Bridgen at the Museum of English Rural Life; Christopher Bowles at Scottish Borders Council for his help; Peter Herring for very useful discussions about peat cutting on Bodmin; Dr Chris Smart for library services; the staff of the Devon and Somerset Record Offices; Sue Dymond for help with water meadows; Dave Cowley (RCAHMS Scottish sheep stells) for helping us to understand the 'Scottish Connection'.

Others have provided much needed and appreciated technical assistance: Brian Cox for his photographs of the peat cutting spades; Matt Sully for assisting with digital mapping and aerial photography.

We would like to thank John and Deidre Hodgson for patiently helping us to develop the maps and reconstruction drawings. Without John's attention to detail so much of the insights given by the archaeology would be left uncommunicated.

We would like to mention several individuals who have an effortless knowledge of Exmoor, and a perspective on that knowledge: to Hugh Thomas for his help drawn from a lifetime's knowledge of Exmoor, its estates and farms; to Graham Wills for kindly agreeing to read and comment on the text and for quietly inspiring the rest of us.

Finally, Robin Taylor and all his colleagues in the publishing department at English Heritage for bringing this book to you.

FOREWORD

This important and interesting book is funded, and being published by English Heritage.

The book is based on an archaeological survey of Exmoor carried out as part of English Heritage's National Mapping Programme. This involved the detailed analysis of thousands of aerial photographs to identify and interpret archaeological sites from the air.

The most striking revelation was the sheer extent and dramatic influence that farming and reclamation have had on Exmoor's landscape. The book, therefore, offers an archaeological insight into how people – farmers and landowners – have shaped Exmoor over the last centuries.

My family has been associated with Exmoor since 1155 when Henry II gave them a grant of land at Landkey near Barnstaple. Since then, through judicious marriages, they acquired more and more land stretching from Barnstaple to Minehead and further into Somerset and down to Exeter. The estate was given by Sir Richard Acland to the National Trust in 1944.

Sir Thomas Acland was warden of the royal forest of Exmoor and was under bidder when Mr Knight acquired the land from the Crown at the beginning of the 19th century. So the agricultural practices of the family and the tenant farmers at that time must have had a considerable impact on the archaeology of Exmoor as we find it today.

Life on Exmoor has always been, and remains, tough. When my elder brother first came to the Somerset longhouse, which my wife and I bought in 1990 and which was originally part of the Acland estates, he commented that it was not just a question of living on Exmoor, but a question of survival! It is not quite as bad as that, and the wonderful scenery makes up for a lot, but Exmoor continues to present a real challenge to modern farmers as it did to those who farmed here in the past.

Exmoor farmers remain tough, resilient and enterprising. The challenge of harsh winters and heavy rainfall have been met by sheer resourcefulness and also by the application of innovative technologies, such as sophisticated water management systems or the Sutherland plough. Today modern equipment has been a great asset, leading to a marked reduction in manpower.

The archaeology described in this book is evidence of the achievement of farmers in the past, many of whose lives were never documented or their methods written down. Modern farmers continue to face considerable challenges but they also have the responsibility to maintain the beauty and the amenities of Exmoor. The precious moorland must be maintained. I am glad to be President of the Exmoor Society, the purposes of which are preserving the beauties of Exmoor, while encouraging hill farmers and sensible investment in small businesses and affordable housing that does not damage the landscape that we all love and admire. These efforts too will add their own layer to the archaeology of Exmoor.

Sir Anthony Acland KG

PREFACE

This river [Exe] hath his head and springeth first in a weely [poor] and barren ground named Exmore, neere unto Severn sea, a great part whereof is counted within Sommersetshire.

(Camden 1610)

This book explores how farmers have gone about taming and making productive the beguiling yet harsh environment of Exmoor. It is a story of hill farming; a story told from an archaeological perspective taking as a primary strand of evidence the information contained on aerial photographs. The focus of the book is the battle – and it is a battle – to make the wastes and moorland of this upland landscape as productive as possible.

The central concept, therefore, is reclamation. 'Reclamation', along with words like 'improvement' and 'taming' suggest a bettering of a condition. It is a Victorian term borne out of the notion that the land was there to be bettered; to be made productive. As such the reclamation of Exmoor is often seen purely as a 19th-century phenomenon, and because of that a great deal of research has focused on the 'improving' of the former royal forest that lies at the centre of Exmoor.

The landscape of today does indeed owe a great deal to this period. In fact the years between 1820 and 1870 did more to shape the area of the high moor than any other time since the Bronze Age. Nonetheless, attempts to improve the high ground of Exmoor have a much deeper history and reflect the efforts of pioneer farmers from the medieval period onwards, so this book, as well as setting out the narrative of 19th-century reclamation, seeks the earlier origins of 'reclamation', not only by the great estates that came to own so much of Exmoor, but by the individual farmers, some of whom, in Hoskins' words (1954) 'farmed in complete isolation', ploughing a lonely furrow with only the eagles and ravens to keep them company.

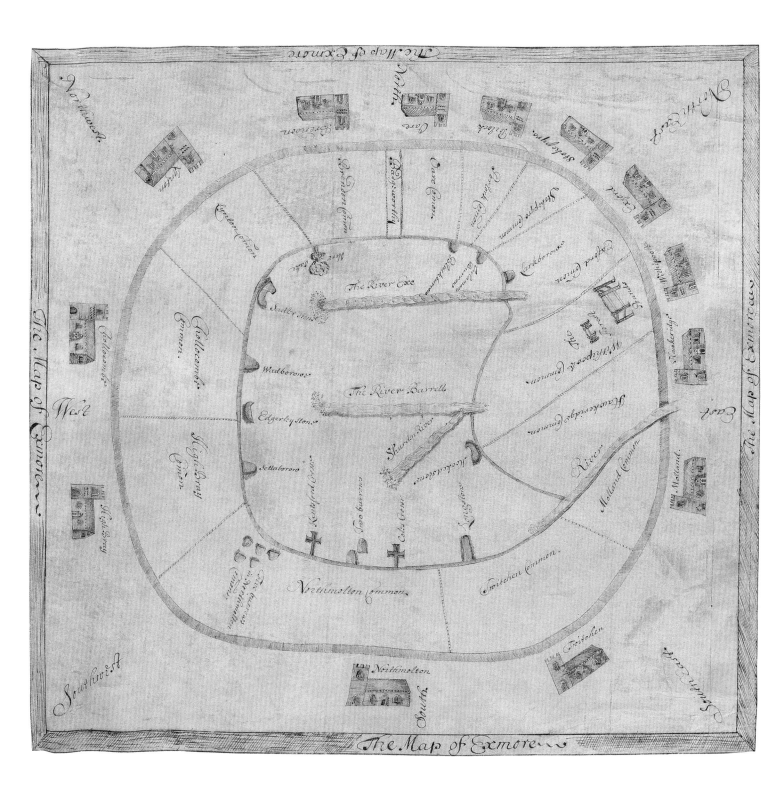

Introduction

This book explains how hill farmers have reclaimed the wastes of Exmoor. It covers the period from the time of Henry II (1133–1189) until the end of the 19th century and in contrast to previous studies, it looks at reclamation from an archaeological perspective. The validity of this approach originates in the body of information gathered from the examination and analysis of thousands of aerial photographs. This aerial viewpoint gives new insights into the processes that shaped the landscape. The archaeological evidence, mapped and interpreted from the air and on the ground, is also placed in its proper historical context.

Previous studies of Exmoor have been made from largely historical viewpoints: agricultural, economic or local history. Two of these works in particular, Edward MacDermot's (1973) *A History of the Forest of Exmoor* and Charles Orwin's *The Reclamation of Exmoor Forest* (Orwin and Sellick 1970), first published in 1929, are seminal works on the subject. More recent studies, such as Roger Burton's (1989) *The Heritage of Exmoor* and Hazel Eardley-Wilmot's (1990) *Yesterday's Exmoor* have mined local history to add valuable detail and provide a more intimate perspective.

This book, unlike the others, does not have a linear or chronological structure and is not constrained by the boundaries of the former royal forest. Instead it takes as its starting point a map of Exmoor drawn in 1675. The map divides Exmoor into three areas. At the centre is the royal forest; around it are the surrounding commons; and beyond, in an outer ring, are the parishes (represented by their churches) to which the commons belong. Correspondingly, the three main sections of this book will in turn examine the archaeological evidence for reclamation within the former royal forest, assess the impact of reclamation on the exploitation of the commons and examine the role played by the hill farmers of Exmoor as they shaped their own holdings.

Exmoor's topography and character

Exmoor is an upland. It straddles the county boundaries between Devon and Somerset in south-west England. On its northern side it overlooks the Bristol Channel in a series of spectacular hog's back cliffs. To the south it overlooks the undulating lowland of mid-Devon's Culm Measures, towards Dartmoor in the far distance.

In character Exmoor displays none of the austere nature of Dartmoor; rather, it is a soft upland. An oft quoted remark is, 'Dartmoor for grandeur, but Exmoor is sublime.' S H Burton described Exmoor's qualities as follows: 'not in the whole of Britain is there more varied beauty in so small a space as can be found inside the boundaries of the Exmoor National Park' (1969, 9).

The geological complexity and the absence of granite bedrock on Exmoor contribute to its varied topography and landscape character, resulting in Exmoor being very different from the other, better known, south-western moorlands of Dartmoor and Bodmin. Its softer character means that it has offered tempting opportunities for cultivation; a more dynamic, and in that sense, liminal, landscape.

Before about 25 million years ago Exmoor is thought to have formed a continuous plateau or plain along with the area west of Exmoor and mid-Devon. At some point in the mid-Tertiary era Exmoor was separated and lifted along fault lines, forming the high plateaux or 'horst' we know today (Edmonds *et al* 1975, 18; Edwards 2000, 28).

Over half of the National Park is now at an elevation over 300m, dominated by three ridges that divide the landscape in a roughly east to west direction. These landforms are the remains of an extensive plateau now eroded and deeply incised by the valleys or combes of Exmoor's main rivers and tributaries, but still following the alignment of the underlying geology.

Fig 0.1
A late 17th-century map of Exmoor Forest, its boundaries, surrounding commons and parishes. [Courtesy of the National Archives]

These ridges now help to define the characteristic landscape of Exmoor, which comprises rounded hills, long spurs and ridges, divided by narrow and steeply sided combes or valleys. The southern limit of the higher ground is an escarpment, which includes several of Exmoor's larger commons and moors, among them Molland and Anstey, reaching elevations of 350m or more. The central ridge includes the inhospitable, high, wet ground of the Chains and towards the east, Dunkery Hill, with Exmoor's highest point at 519m. The northern ridge forms the coastal cliffs and heaths, overlooking the Bristol Channel, with some of the most remote and inaccessible coastline in England. Exmoor's cliffs have a distinctive profile with long seaward slopes above a small but steep sea cliff at their base (Edwards 2000). The consid-erable height and dramatic nature of the sea cliffs ensure there is very limited access to the shoreline from Combe Martin to Heddon's Mouth and from Countisbury to Glenthorne.

The east of the National Park is dominated by the Brendon Hills, which reach heights of over 400m. As such, there is a range of only 150m or so over most of higher Exmoor, the ridges forming plateaus echoing the Devonian tableland of geological history (Straw 1995; Edwards 2000). In contrast, west Exmoor rarely exceeds 300m in height. It retains a plateau character but, separated from central Exmoor by geological faults and shear zones, has more in common with the lower-lying landscape of central Devon (Straw 1995).

To the north-east, the coastal cliffs between Hurlestone Point and Gore Point are broken by

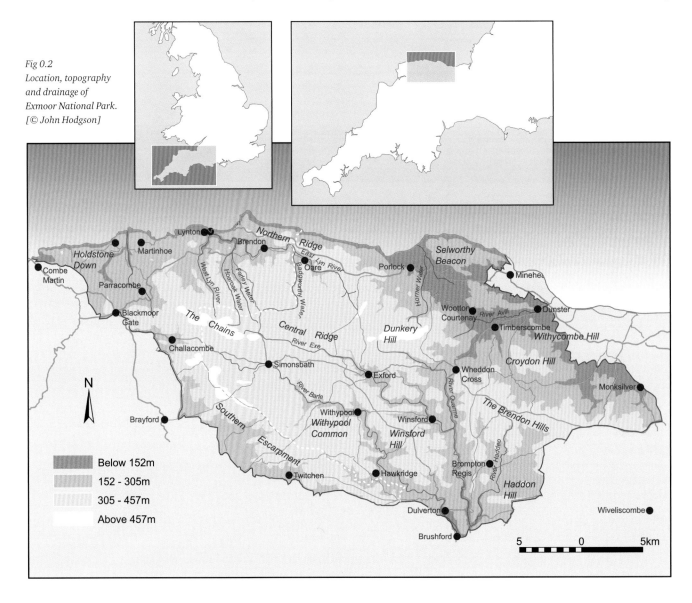

Fig 0.2
Location, topography and drainage of Exmoor National Park.
[© John Hodgson]

the softer mudstones of the Triassic, forming the 3km-long coastal plain of Porlock Bay. Behind the beach is a shingle ridge that separates the beach from a rapidly evolving saltmarsh (Edwards 2000). The low-lying Vale of Porlock remains a relatively well settled, agriculturally productive zone bounded on all sides by upland (Findlay *et al* 1984; Riley and Wilson-North 2001, 3).

Numerous watercourses occupy narrow and steep combes, which incise this upland landscape. They form four main watersheds that divide the moors into compact east-to-west sections (Curtis 1971, 3). The central ridge forms a 'drainage divide'. Those rivers to the north mainly flow in very steep, short courses to the Bristol Channel and those to the south flow along gentler gradients and longer courses to the English Channel, mostly via the rivers Exe and Barle (Edmonds *et al* 1975; Edwards 2000). The main northerly flowing rivers are the West and East Lyn, which reach open water at Lynmouth. Smaller streams include the River Umber, which meets the sea at Combe Martin in the far north-west, the River Heddon, which flows out at Heddon's Mouth, and Horner

Water, which joins the Bristol Channel near Bossington. To the east the River Avill passes through Dunster before meeting the sea near Minehead. The main southerly flowing rivers are the Exe and the Barle, flowing generally east and then to the south on their long journey through Devon to meet the sea at Exmouth (Edwards 2000; Riley and Wilson-North 2001).

A distinctive feature of many of Exmoor's combes or valleys (such as the Barle, Exe and Oare Water) are small natural knolls or mounds. These are formed of outcrops of rock more resistant to river erosion than the softer valley slopes from which they may be separated by geological faults or joints. Over time they have become isolated by erosion to form separate mounds. People have exploited these features because they provide dry ground and shelter; several are occupied by sheepfolds.

The moors of Dartmoor and Bodmin are largely formed from granite which gives them their distinctive rugged and craggy appearance, with prominent tors and areas of surface moor stone. Exmoor's softer character derives from a solid geology dominated by sedimentary rather than igneous rock.

Fig 0.3
Exmoor's geology.
[© John Hodgson]

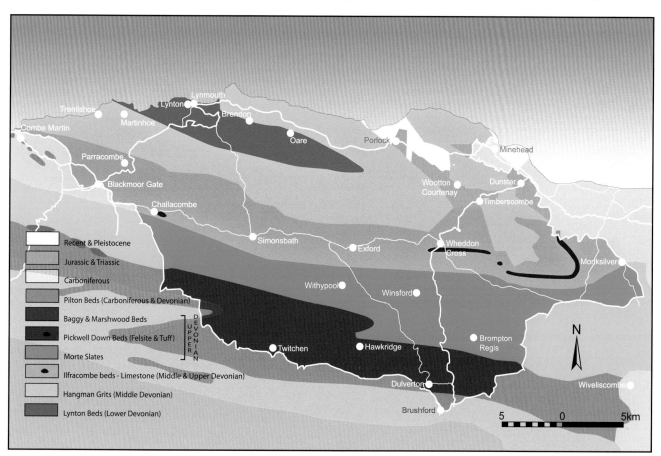

In particular Exmoor is made up of rocks from the Devonian period, laid down between 405 and 355 million years ago. Devonian rocks comprise sandstone or slate. Individual formations are named in two parts, first, after the places at which they are best seen, then the main type of rock of which they are composed (ie sandstone or slate) (Edwards 2000).

The Devonian formations were laid down in dramatically changing conditions as north Devon was covered either by equatorial sandy plains, during which periods Hangman Sandstone was laid down, or inundated by shallow tropical seas, when the oldest Exmoor formations, the Lynton Slates formed, about 350 million years ago (Edwards 2000, 12; Edmonds *et al* 1975).

About 300 million years ago southerly acting geological forces compressed the flat Devonian deposits into large folds or arch-like shapes, creating a range of mountains probably on the scale of the Himalayas. The folds were aligned east to west and Exmoor's three main ridges and rounded hills are eroded stumps of these. The centre of the fold, made up of the Lynton Formation, runs roughly from Lynton to Porlock. To the north the rocks tilt northwards and to the south of it, and over most of Exmoor, the rocks tilt southwards, the formations becoming younger the further from the centre they are (Edwards 2000, 11; 13). The formations range from a few hundred metres to over 1600m thick and the varying thickness and hardness of each formation has shaped each element of Exmoor's distinctive landscape. For instance, the extremely hard sandstone of the Middle Devonian Hangman Grits forms the highest parts of Exmoor and the characteristic coastal formations of the northern escarpment. The centre of Exmoor is defined by belts of the Middle and Upper Devonian Ilfracombe Beds, Upper Devonian Morte Slates and the Pickwell Down Beds (Riley and Wilson-North 2001).

Much younger Triassic and Jurassic deposits are found in areas around the northern and eastern sides of Exmoor, such as the Vale of Porlock, Luccombe, Wootton Courtenay and Minehead. Formed as the north Devon mountain range eroded, gravels and clays, such as the Luccombe Breccias, spread out filling up valleys and plains alongside beds of river-tumbled rounded pebbles. Later, thick deposits of Mercia Mudstone (Keuper Marl) were laid down, filling up geological faults, forming the low ground of the Vale of Porlock.

One of the most recent formations occurred during the last ice age, roughly 2 million to 10,000 years ago, in a period known as the Quaternary. Although probably not covered by sheet ice, the effects of freeze and thaw affected Exmoor. One of the most widespread deposits on Exmoor, known as 'head' (a mix of ice-cracked angular local rock with clay), was laid down probably during a 'cold snap' and covered slopes as it spread during repeated thaws and refreezing. A skin of head material covers much of Exmoor's Devonian bones, in often surprisingly thick layers (Edwards 2000, 16).

Land use

Of Exmoor's 69,280 hectares, 19,000 (*c* 27 per cent) are moorland, 38,000 (55 per cent) are farmland and the remaining *c* 12,000 hectares (*c* 18 per cent) is largely composed of woodland, a third of which is classified as 'ancient'. The main block of open moorland runs from west to east across the National Park, from Challacombe Common and the Chains to Dunkery Hill. This area includes much of the former royal forest of Exmoor and some of the neighbouring commons (Riley and Wilson-North 2001, 5). Other smaller areas of moor lie around the former royal forest on the commons.

The surrounding enclosed farmland seems to have been made in the medieval period but continued to develop and expand through the post medieval. Today, Exmoor remains a hill-farming region with sheep and beef cattle the main outputs, although a few dairy farms are located in the milder, more sheltered fringes of the National Park. This farming regime has preserved a varied landscape of moorland, semi-improved and improved pasture. The exception to this is in the arable land of the Vale of Porlock, which is limited in area but of very good quality, and in the past has produced high yields of cereals, vining peas, linseed, swedes, potatoes and grapes.

The settlement pattern is one of small dispersed farmsteads, hamlets and villages, which are mainly concentrated on the lower slopes or in the river valleys. This pattern is an ancient one and originated in the medieval period and has changed little since. The larger settlements lie on the fringes of the National Park and are found on the coast – at Dunster, Lynton and Porlock – and on the south side at Dulverton.

Soils

Exmoor's varied geology, landform and climate have resulted in a wide range of soils, which contribute to the diverse vegetation and land use. This can be seen in the contrast over a distance of 20km between the productive agricultural soils on the permo-triassic rocks of the Vale of Porlock and the blanket bogs of the Chains, with peat deposits up to nearly 3m in depth.

The soils of the south-west of England are generally poorly suited to arable farming and most of Exmoor is no exception (Findlay *et al* 1984). The parent Devonian rocks are covered by locally derived head with only the most superficial levels degrading to form soils (Findlay *et al* 1984; Maltby 1995). Exmoor's soils developed from frost-shattered material deposited in periglacial conditions in the postglacial Holocene period, approximately 10,000 years ago when Exmoor would have resembled a 'steppe' landscape.

As the climate warmed, vegetation colonised the land and by the late Mesolithic (8000–4000 BC) deciduous forest on loamy brown soils came to dominate. By late prehistory woodland survived only in sheltered combes and around spring heads, and blanket peat was forming across the uplands (Fyfe 2011).

The cause and rate of deforestation, waterlogging and peat bog formation is still much debated, but the character of the uplands and valley slopes, dominated by peat deposits of varying depths, probably has its origin in the Bronze and Iron Ages. However, human activity, particularly tree clearance, may have been a contributing factor from the late Neolithic (c 2000 BC). It is certain that tree loss coincides with the emergence of the first man-made ritual monuments, such as stone settings, and clearance cairns may be evidence of dramatic reorganisation of the landscape for hunting and grazing (Fyfe 2011; Gillings *et al* 2010; Maltby 1995).

Whatever the cause, tree loss led to a loss of fertility, increased waterlogging, podzolisation (*see* Glossary) and the subsequent establishment of acid-soil-loving and aquatic or semi-aquatic plants. Exmoor's landscape of upland heath, moor and bog was created at this time. The main zone of peat formation follows the central plateau from the Chains to Exe Plain, but the deposits of variable depth indicate that peat developed at different speeds in different locations. Thinner blanket peat occurs on upland areas above 400m and downslope the peat

becomes thinner and often merges with soils of peaty surface horizons, very acid permeable podzols, stagnohumic gleys and thin iron-pan stagnopodzols (*see* Glossary), known locally as 'black ram' on upper valley slopes (Edmonds *et al* 1975, 104; Maltby 1995). On Exmoor these soils occur in Exmoor Forest, Dunkery and Winsford Hills, Molland and Withypool Common.

Changes in historic land use have also probably had an enduring effect on Exmoor's soils and vegetation. From the Early Medieval period (410–1066) onwards, protection of the uplands as a royal forest is likely to have resulted in the management regime known as agistment, the summer grazing of the forest by sheep and cattle. Moorland vegetation, such as heather, cannot tolerate heavy grazing and, consequently, it is assumed that intensive grazing over much of the forest, at least from the 16th century (and probably earlier), led to a landscape dominated by purple moor grass (*molinia careulea*) and deer-grass (*trichophorum caespitosum*). A clear division between soils dominated by purple moor grass and those dominated by heather is still visible between the former royal forest and the commons to the north, despite a common geology (Maltby 1995).

Post-medieval land use probably had little impact on the development of peat. Despite deciduous purple moor grass potentially being beneficial for the formation of peat, the grazing pressures and incidental manuring effects of agistment and regular swaling (*see* Glossary) did not encourage peat formation. In contrast, following the enclosure of Exmoor at the start of the 19th century, the practise of agistment was much reduced and the development of peat greatly increased, 'a dramatic illustration of the importance of land use regimes on the ecological dynamics not only of vegetation but of peat formation' (Maltby 1995, 36).

Unsurprisingly the reclamation strategies employed in the 19th century also had a profound effect on moorland soils. The processes employed included paring and burning, liming, half ploughing and reseeding the moorland with more desirable seed mixes. Focusing largely on the stagnohumic gleys and stagnopodzols of the gentle south-facing slopes, which were more amenable to mechanical improvement, these methods succeeded in creating new soil horizons over the original peaty soils from which it was formed, and through new types of vegetation, sustained drainage and improvement (such as liming), maintained them.

Climate

As throughout the south-west, the climate of Exmoor is influenced greatly by altitude, aspect and proximity to the sea. The general pattern is one of warm summers and cool winters with higher than average rainfall. Only in a few areas of the south-west is annual rainfall below 1,000mm, but the uplands of Exmoor regularly exceed 2,000mm, the rain falling mostly in the autumn and winter. Further to the east the moderating influence of westerly mild and moist maritime winds is lessened. The uplands of Exmoor have some of the lowest annual average temperatures in the south-west. Winters can be cold. Despite potentially having a growing season of up to 225 days a year, the potential for agricultural improvement is limited by the cool temperatures and moist environment of the upland. Snow, particularly drifting snow, can be a serious challenge for livestock farmers on Exmoor, and is a real danger at key times, such as lambing (Findlay *et al* 1984).

Fig 0.4
The royal forest of Exmoor, showing its varying size through the medieval period. [© John Hodgson]

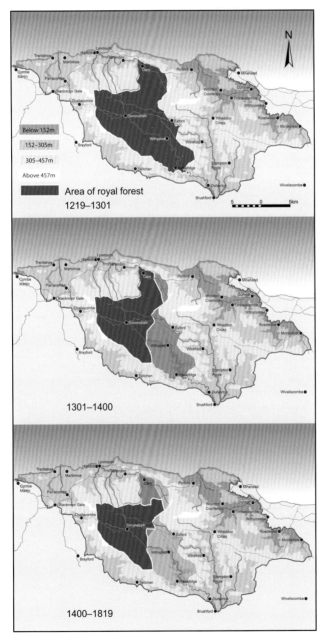

Thematic background – farming from the earliest times

Exmoor's moorlands contain exceptionally well preserved archaeological remains and relict landscapes reflecting the occupation of the area since the last ice age. The moorland has preserved – by virtue of not being successfully converted into farmland – a deep and rare narrative of settlement and activity over this great span of time. There is also an irony in that the attempts to 'reclaim' the moorlands – had they been successful – would have effaced the evidence for this narrative. Because many of the attempts to improve the waste ended in failure, they have become another chapter in its history, and perhaps one of the most important episodes.

People have occupied Exmoor since the late Mesolithic period some 8,000 years ago. These early hunter gatherers began the long process of managing the landscape by clearing forest glades to encourage wild animals for hunting. These early killing grounds no doubt became important places, but it seems unlikely that the people who created them saw this in any way other than survival. Later, in the Neolithic and Bronze Age, monuments were built to appropriate the landscape, and many of these standing stones and other sites can still be found on the remote moorland. Little fields were laid out across much of the upland; arable farming, pastoralism and meadow management were practised and small settlements, of groups of two or three round houses, grew up from which Bronze Age communities could grow their cereal crops and look after their livestock (Riley and Wilson-North 2001).

These activities could be seen by some as reclamation, but they are not in the spirit of it. Prehistoric people practised a subsistence way of life that seems, from the archaeological evidence, to have been relatively adaptive and flexible. On Exmoor, the evidence for prehistoric settlement and farming gives the impression that there was 'room' in the landscape. More recent reclamation was about making unproductive land productive and pushing the frontiers of cultivation into the 'waste'. These are relatively modern concepts and are at variance with what we know of prehistoric (and even medieval) farming practice. What prehistoric and medieval farmers had in common was that any enclosure of the waste seems to have been relatively piecemeal, practised within a subsistence economy in a marginal landscape. This was the case even during the lifetime of the royal forest, in the early medieval to medieval periods (410–1540).

During the later prehistoric periods, as the climate deteriorated, there seems to have been an increasing reliance on livestock. By the early medieval period the farming practices of the prehistoric had given way or evolved into a sophisticated system of convertible husbandry, in which land was subject to strict rotation. In the medieval period the climate improved and population levels increased, so that farmers once again turned to more marginal areas. On and around Exmoor land was pressed into arable production, and even steep north-facing slopes were ploughed. Even at this time, farming remained a subsistence practice with surpluses sold through local markets. It was only later that farmers set out to grow a specific surplus to sell on. That is not to say that large areas were not reclaimed. In fact the extension of medieval farms into the margins of the moors as well as the medieval ploughing of the moorlands must have transformed the landscape at the time. Central to these episodes was the royal forest (Section 1) and the commons (Section 2) that surrounded it. The royal forest probably originated in Anglo-Saxon times and throughout the medieval period its size and influence fluctuated.

Around the royal forest were commons, many of which remain as unenclosed moorland today. Their role and relationship with the forest was fundamental in shaping Exmoor.

Fig 0.5
Exmoor National Park, showing the royal forest at its centre (28), with the surrounding commons. The map differentiates between commons that were enclosed by act of parliament, and those that remain 'common'. [© John Hodgson]

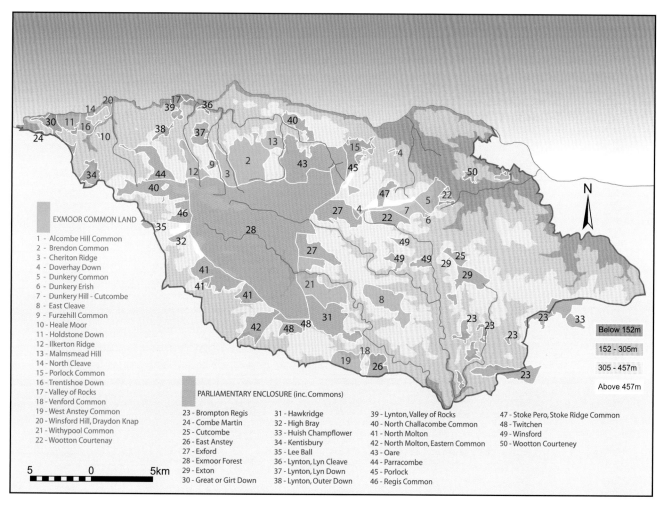

EXMOOR COMMON LAND

1 - Alcombe Hill Common
2 - Brendon Common
3 - Cheriton Ridge
4 - Doverhay Down
5 - Dunkery Common
6 - Dunkery Erish
7 - Dunkery Hill - Cutcombe
8 - East Cleave
9 - Furzehill Common
10 - Heale Moor
11 - Holdstone Down
12 - Ilkerton Ridge
13 - Malmsmead Hill
14 - North Cleave
15 - Porlock Common
16 - Trentishoe Down
17 - Valley of Rocks
18 - Venford Common
19 - West Anstey Common
20 - Winsford Hill, Draydon Knap
21 - Withypool Common
22 - Wootton Courtenay

PARLIAMENTARY ENCLOSURE (inc. Commons)

23 - Brompton Regis
24 - Combe Martin
25 - Cutcombe
26 - East Anstey
27 - Exford
28 - Exmoor Forest
29 - Exton
30 - Great or Girt Down
31 - Hawkridge
32 - High Bray
33 - Huish Champflower
34 - Kentisbury
35 - Lee Ball
36 - Lynton, Lyn Cleave
37 - Lynton, Lyn Down
38 - Lynton, Outer Down
39 - Lynton, Valley of Rocks
40 - North Challacombe Common
41 - North Molton
42 - North Molton, Eastern Common
43 - Oare
44 - Parracombe
45 - Porlock
46 - Regis Common
47 - Stoke Pero, Stoke Ridge Common
48 - Twitchen
49 - Winsford
50 - Wootton Courteney

Below 152m
152 - 305m
305 - 457m
Above 457m

5   0   5km

Case study
Aerial archaeology and the National Mapping Programme

Archaeologists became aware of the value of aerial photography in the 1920s. A new breed of professional archaeologists, such as O G S Crawford, applied methods of aerial observation, interpretation and mapping, which had been developed during the First World War, to archaeology. It took until the 1960s for the value of aerial archaeology to be fully recognised, and it was not until the 1980s that the RCHME (Royal Commission on the Historical Monuments of England) had a formal policy in place for their routine use (RCHME 1960; Barber 2011). From this background the RCHME developed the National Mapping Programme (NMP) in the early 1990s and it now continues under the management of English Heritage.

The broad aim of NMP is to 'enhance the understanding of past human settlement by providing primary information and synthesis for all archaeological sites and landscapes visible on aerial photographs or other airborne remote sensed data', dating from the Neolithic period to the 20th century (Horne 2011). Its great strength is that it is a national programme with standardised methods of recording historic features, although inevitably it responds to local archaeological variations.

NMP was originally designed to exploit the largely untapped potential of existing collections of aerial photographs for studying buried archaeological remains, as well as upstanding sites and structures. However, it has increasingly become a tool for both the protection of the historic environment as well as research. The scope of its methodology has been especially significant when mapping in protected landscapes, such as National Parks and Areas of Outstanding Natural Beauty. Now, new remote sensing techniques, such as LiDAR (Light Detection and Ranging, see Glossary; Crutchley and Crow 2009), are increasingly being consulted and interpreted in the same way as traditional aerial photographs, further expanding the potential of this important tool.

NMP makes use of a range of aerial photographs from different sources. It takes advantage of ongoing aerial reconnaissance by English Heritage aerial photographers, who capture up-to-date oblique aerial photographs for monitoring the condition of known monuments, as well as identifying and recording newly discovered sites. It also uses the millions of vertical and oblique aerial photographs of the English landscape that exist in archives such as the English Heritage Archive in Swindon, and local collections held by local authority Historic Environment Records. Some photographs date from the early days of aerial photography, but most have been taken since the Second World War. Many are not taken for archaeological purposes, but when analysed by specially trained aerial photograph interpreters can provide a record of more recent landscape change as well as revealing more ancient aspects of the country through its landscape archaeology.

Fig 0.6
Aerial photograph interpreters are trained to distinguish archaeological sites and landscape features from non-archaeological features. Using a stereoscope to view vertical aerial photographs gives the interpreter a three dimensional overview of the landscape.

By the early 19th century 'improvement' and 'reclamation' were carried out in response to a range of social and, economic factors. Threats to the security of the national food supply caused by the Napoleonic wars, increased population levels and the Industrial Revolution all meant that there was a drive to make unproductive land productive. Technical innovations, the use of machines and the advance of the railway network also combined to make the remoteness of certain areas less of an obstacle. Exmoor was at the centre of this imperative and in the same way that Victorian reclamation culminated on Exmoor, so too did reclamation on Exmoor culminate in the 19th century.

The National Mapping Programme on Exmoor

The NMP survey of Exmoor National Park was carried out between 2007 and 2009. During this time more than 10,000 aerial photographs were examined and over 2,000 previously unrecognised archaeological sites were recorded, with the information for over 800 known monuments enhanced.

The aerial view allowed an unprecedented insight into Exmoor's uplands, revealing some unrecorded sites but, as importantly, allowing a landscape-scale perception of its historic character. Historic vertical photographs provided new insights into the changing face of the moors and their environs in the 20th century as well as the landscape legacy of Victorian agricultural improvement. Aerial photographs really do show the impact of people in shaping what is often viewed as an unspoilt landscape.

Exmoor's subtle archaeology presents a particular challenge to the aerial archaeologist and has necessitated maximising the potential of the resources available, such as using photographs taken at different times of the year to exploit variations in vegetation, light conditions and water levels, or using and comparing photographs taken at different dates.

Upstanding archaeological sites – in the form of earthworks – are the most commonly recorded sites visible from the air. The NMP survey has been able to record the extent and morphology of thousands of upstanding archaeological features, such as the remains of relict medieval field systems, Victorian drainage schemes and even the slight remains of shallow peat cuttings or turf pits made by generations of Exmoor farmers.

Taken as a whole, the NMP survey of Exmoor provides an invaluable tool for managing the historic environment. In addition it will lead research into aspects of Exmoor's past by recording the extent of surviving archaeology. At a deeper level, it changes our perception of how much effort and determination was involved in shaping Exmoor's landscape.

Section 1

The royal forest

The origins of the royal forest

Exmoor National Park, like much of Britain's uplands, maintains a precious archaeological legacy stretching back to the late Mesolithic era, roughly 8,000 years ago. Many of the earthwork monuments on Exmoor owe their survival to the remoteness and harsh nature of the environment, which often provided a formidable obstacle to later attempts to farm the landscape; their survival also owes a great deal to Exmoor's former status as a royal forest. This status protected Exmoor from the ravages of intensive agricultural exploitation that transformed much of southern England in the medieval period. But how did Exmoor become a royal forest, and why were royal forests such special places?

It may in fact have been a lack of 'specialness', at least to the early medieval farmer, which originally set Exmoor apart. By the time of the Saxon expansion into the south-west, in around the 8th century AD, Exmoor was perceived as a 'waste': an agriculturally unproductive area which belonged to no-one, and so in some senses, to everyone. The absence of human activity would have allowed undomesticated animals to thrive, and the quality of the hunting may have attracted people to the area. In this way Exmoor probably became the demesne of the Saxon kings, and following the Norman Conquest, the property of the Crown.

However, the precise age of the forest as an institution is unclear. By the 12th century Exmoor was one of 67 royal forests in England which 'were so ancient as no record or history doth make any mention of their erection or beginnings' (Lord Chief Justice Coke, quoted in MacDermot 1973, 1). Nonetheless *Exmore*, as it is often named in the surviving documents, was well established by the mid-11th century and the forest almost certainly had an Anglo-Saxon precursor.

The term 'forest' is first mentioned in Domesday Book, the Saxons having no word with the same legal significance or meaning. However, hunting for sport was a noble pastime in the Saxon period, and indications of stock management exist. For instance, the word 'hays', from the Old English *haga*, has been interpreted as describing woodland enclosures created to preserve deer for hunting, an early form of resource management (Hooke 1989). On Saxon Exmoor, the existence of something approaching a forest in practical terms, if not name, is implied as Domesday mentions three 'foresters' who 'held half a hide in Withypool' (Exon. Domesday, Domesday Book vol 1, p 443). It is therefore probable that the Anglo-Saxon kings exercised control over hunting on Exmoor, although possibly as landowners rather than royalty; forest law in all its complexity and (supposed) cruelty was a Norman introduction (Rackham 1998).

It is now widely appreciated that 'forest' is a legal term, and unlike the term 'park', does not necessarily describe a particular kind of landscape or vegetation. Palaeo-environmental studies indicate that Exmoor was last fully wooded probably in the late Mesolithic period (*c* 8,000–4,000 BC) and clearance for pasture began towards the end of the Neolithic (4,000–2,000 BC). Other than in sheltered combes, upland Exmoor has been largely treeless since the Bronze Age, with any surviving woodland finally cleared in the Iron Age (Fyfe 2011; Fyfe *et al* 2003). The term 'forest' more properly describes an area where natural resources have been reserved for the Crown. There were wooded forests in England, many of which were private estates rather than royal holdings and so more properly called 'chases', but treeless upland or moorland forests were much greater in area, if fewer in number. At their height, there were as many as 74 upland forests and chases in England (Winchester 2004).

However, few of these upland forests were royal demesne and therefore most were not subject to forest law.

An evocative view of royal forests is summarised by Rackham (1998, 65): 'to the medievals a forest was a place of deer, not a place of trees'. So to at least some parts of society a forest was a kind of unfenced hunting ground where deer were kept 'for sport and for the table' (Rackham 1998, 130). The 'beasts of the forest' preserved by forest law variously included red deer, fallow deer and until the mid-14th century, roe deer, but wild boar were also reserved for the king and in rare instances, other animals such as hare could be protected. In *A treatise and discourse of the lawes of the forrest* Manwood describes the key features of a royal forest as:

1 **Vert**: preserving the woodland vegetation for the game;

2 **Venison**: preserving the principle game species;

3 **Forest Law**: to uphold the Lord's right to the vert and venison, replacing the common law;

4 The appointment of a Forester and other officials.

These were meant to ensure that forests were 'the better … preserved and kept for a place of recreation and pastime meete for the Royal dignity of a Prince' (Manwood 1615, quoted in Winchester 2004).

However, despite numerous references in the forest court rolls to presentments for illegal hunting, there is limited evidence for any kind of royal presence on Exmoor. In the 13th and 14th centuries some lands were held around Exmoor in 'serjeanty', a form of land-holding given in return for a specific service. In this instance the service was typically to provide the king with 'three barbed arrows when he shall hunt in the forest of Exemore' (MacDermot 1973, 29), but there are no records of any king actually visiting Exmoor in person. The closest it would appear that royalty got to Exmoor was to send huntsmen or servants to take deer for them, as is recorded as happening on Exmoor in 1315 for Edward II.

It seems that the most significant, if possibly less glamorous function of a royal forest, was one of income generation. Deer were a relatively rare and prestigious resource, but pasture was extensive and cheap (Winchester 2004, 25).

The changing forest

The size of the Saxon forest and the adjoining commons, which were probably developing at around the same time, are unknown (MacDermot 1973, 2). The relationship between the commons and the medieval forest is examined in Section 2. By the late 12th century, the forest probably reached its greatest size, extending from the coast in the north to Dulverton and the River Yeo in the south, with the River Bray defining its western limits and Porlock and Horner Water its eastern edge (MacDermot 1973; Siraut 2009).

Fig 1.1
The boundary of the royal forest of Exmoor fluctuated during the 13th and 14th centuries, its final extent becoming more or less established in the 15th century (based on MacDermot 1973 and Gillard 2002).
[© John Hodgson]

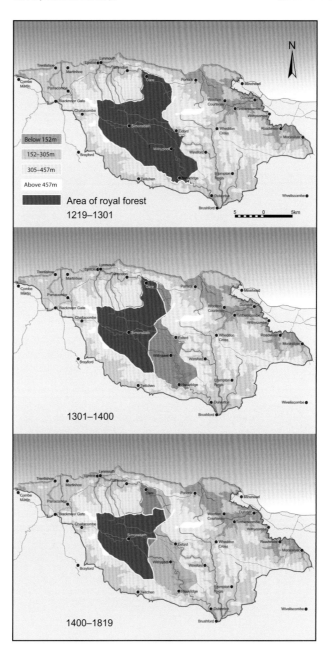

Despite crossing Exmoor, the county boundary between Devonshire and Somersetshire may have been undefined within the forest, the waste itself effectively forming the border; as the forest was an unsettled waste there was no great need to mark the boundary (MacDermot 1973, 2; 14). Equally, as a separate bailiwick, under the authority of neither the sheriff of Devon nor of Somerset, Exmoor was 'in a legal sense', in neither county (Chanter 1907, 269). In 1204, however, a charter of King John disafforested all the parishes of Devon, which in 1207 returned the bounds of the royal forests 'as far as the metes of the old regards of Dertemore and Exemore as the regards were in the time of King Henry the first', in other words, restoring the royal forests of Devon to their older limits. For this the men of Devon reimbursed the king handsomely, paying a thousand marks (£666 13s 4d) for the privilege of no longer living under forest law. It is uncertain exactly how much of Devon had previously been forested, but it may have been a substantial area, possibly equating to those estates that continued to owe service to the forest Swainmote court from the 16th to the 19th centuries (MacDermot 1973, 195–6; Gillard 2002, 31). It may amount to as much as another 150,000 acres (Chanter 1907, 292–3). A perambulation (*see* Glossary) of 1207 fixed the western boundary of the forest as the line which later became the Devon county boundary with the royal forest, until its sale in 1819, although mapmakers up to the middle of the 17th century, such as Speed and Camden, continue to show the county boundary running north–south across the middle of Exmoor (Chanter 1907, 274).

However, the expansion of royal forests continued apace. The royal forest of Exmoor, now solely within Somerset, continued to expand under King John, building upon the earlier expansions of Henry II until it encompassed an area including the present parishes of Hawkridge, Withypool, Exmoor forest, Oare Culbone, Porlock, Luccombe, Stoke Pero, Cutcombe, Exford, Winsford and Dulverton, plus parts of Selworthy, Wootton Courtenay and Exton (MacDermot 1973, 114). Following many complaints and grievances from the people about abuses of forest law by forest officials, these expansions were unmade by Magna Carta in 1215, when all the eastern parishes were disafforested and the shape of the royal forest, and ultimately the future parish of Exmoor, was finally established.

Perambulations

The eastern boundary of the forest within Somerset was established and maintained by perambulation. Originating as a walk to define and maintain an estate or property boundary, some perambulations were later written as appendices to Anglo-Saxon charters, becoming legal documents for the conveyance of a piece of land or estate. These documents have provided historians with a valuable tool in defining the changing shape and extent of Exmoor (Rackham 1998, 9). The perambulations had the important function of using landscape features, both natural and archaeological, to describe the extent of the land being enclosed or defined, by clearly describing the boundary by moving from point to point. With a few exceptions, such as legal forests and monastic estates, the use of perambulations generally faded in England after the Norman Conquest, although a few communities continue to 'beat the bounds' of their town or parish today.

The first perambulation of the Somerset boundary of Exmoor forest has been traced to the early 13th century, in the years following a charter of the child-king Edward III in 1217, which effectively disafforested all areas forested by Richard I and King John, reducing their areas to that claimed by Henry II (MacDermot 1973). A special commission of 1219 directed the sheriff of Somerset and Dorset to carry out perambulations in his counties, directing that four 'good and lawful men' chose '12 of the more lawful and trusty knights' of the county to 'cause to be made a true perambulation between those parts of the aforesaid counties which aught to be disafforested, and those parts which will remain forest' (MacDermot 1973, 116).

The number of marker locations described in perambulations varies from place to place, but for Exmoor the 1219 perambulation is as follows (modern placenames, where known, are stated in square brackets):

ESSEMORE. The Lord King's Forest of Essemore begins from Corsneshet [Cosgate] and stretches to Whitestone [probably the Fifstones boundary stones mentioned in later perambulations, at the Oare-Culbone boundary on Yenworthy Common], from the top of Whitestone to Hauekescumeshead [Hawkcombe Head], from Hauekescumeshead by the top of the hill to Osmundesburgh

[Alderman's Barrow], from Osmundesburgh to the little Eisse [the little Exe, either the stream in Sparcombe/Orchard Bottom or Alcombe Water], from the little Eisse to the great Eisse [the River Exe] by the course of the water, by the course of the great Eisse to la Rode [Road Castle], and from thence to Ernesburg [possibly Herne's Barrow on Court Hill] by the great way, from Ernesburg by the great way to Wamburg [the Wambarrows on Winsford Hill], from Wamburg to Langeston [the Longstone inscribed stone near Spire Cross, possibly the Caratacus Stone], from Langeston to Mageldene [unidentified, possibly a combe head near Mounsey Hill Gate] ... and from thence by the great way [a highway or track] between the two Eisseweis [probably the manors of Ashway Ashwick and Ashway Ford] to the water of Bergel, and along the water of Bergel [the Barle] to [where] Donekesbroch [Danes Brook] falls into Bergel. And from these bounds towards the West as far as Devon is the ancient forest, and towards the East is outside the forest. All the other woods, which have been afforested, have been afforested since the coronation of the Lord King Henry grandfather of the Lord King Henry son of the Lord King John.

(After MacDermot 1973, 117–18)

Various expansions and contractions of the area considered as afforested came and went over the next 80 years or so, with foresters continuing to abuse their position and the concept of forest law for their own gain. New perambulations took place, were revoked and took place again, but the legal boundary as set out in the perambulation of 1300, which excluded Withypool and Hawkridge from the forest, proved to be more or less durable, and has survived largely in the boundary of Exmoor parish we know it today (MacDermot 1973).

Fig 1.2
As prominent features in the landscape, prehistoric burial mounds were regularly incorporated into perambulations around the royal forest. After enclosure, the boundary of the Knights' estate followed the same route as the later perambulations, slighting many forest markers, as here at Setta Barrow.
[NMR SS 7238/4 (21075/18) 09-Feb-2001]

The medieval royal forest: grazing, gathering, government and grievances

In the Anglo-Saxon period the natural resources of Exmoor were probably exploited by those living in its hinterlands. The name Exmoor is itself first recorded in the 12th century, but that the moor had economic significance beyond hunting is implied by an indirect reference in the Domesday Book entry for Molland to 'the pastures of the moor' (Rackham 1998, 309). The deer were perceived as the most valuable resource of the forest, but the taking of game was restricted to the king, his officials or those favourites to whom he granted his favour. Other less glamorous forest resources, however, were arguably more valuable and had a much greater impact on the lives of the locals and officials alike. In 1184 laws called the 'Assizes of the Forest' were introduced, which extended forest law protection to the 'vert', meaning any woodland and vegetation which may provide game cover. This meant that people could often no longer collect the fuel they had been accustomed to, nor graze livestock, nor extend farmland without either payment or by breaking the law. To make matters more difficult the forest boundary fluctuated and forest officials often used this confusion as an excuse to apply forest law well beyond its legal boundary, and affect people in their own homes and farmsteads.

The forest courts: the court of Eyre

The boundary of the royal forest and the remit of forest law were clearly of great interest to those who lived in the surrounding manors. After disafforestment the lords of the Devon manors to the west of the forest boundary could permit their tenants to graze livestock, cultivate their commons and cut turves as they pleased. Those to the east, however, remained subject to the full force of forest law as interpreted by the forester and under-foresters, the officials of the forest courts.

It is from the accounts of the forest courts that we get much of our understanding of how the resources of the forest were used. The term 'forest' itself derives from the latin *foris*, which, depending on context, means 'outside' or 'abroad', in this instance outside the common law. Exmoor came under the remit of two courts, the court of Eyre and the Swainmote court.

The 13th-century court of Eyre was an itinerant court in which the king's justices visited the various afforested counties around the country. In general this court visited a county no more frequently than once every 7 years, often much less frequently, and for Somerset, the court was often held at Ilchester. It was primarily concerned with offences against the resources of the royal forest, and court records are split accordingly into three sections: pleas against the Venison, pleas against the Vert and the Regard of Exemore.

Offences 'against the venison', in the form of poaching, were surprisingly rare. Pleas against the vert were rarely recorded in detail, but the 'vert' was defined as vegetation and undergrowth that provided cover for the 'venison and beasts of the Forest'. Furze and bracken was gathered for animal feed and even building material, or to be burnt with what wood there was to be gathered. Disturbing it was punishable by a fine.

The 'Regard' of a royal forest was the inspection of the woods and lands within the forest subject to forest law, which was made every 3 years by officers called 'regarders', and crimes against the regard included such offences as assarting (clearing the forest) and growing crops, purprestures (making enclosures), waste (cutting wood) and turbary (turf cutting) without a licence (MacDermot 1973, 22, 81, 90). Turf was cut primarily for fuel and sometimes used for building temporary fencing, but turbaries would also cause disturbance to the deer and were therefore authorised only under licence. For instance, in 1270 Hillary de Munceaux was fined 'half a mark' for cutting wood without a licence, and in the same year seven Exford and Withypool men were fined for making illegal turbaries (Siraut 2009, 61–2; MacDermot 1973, 90). Turf could be cut legally on the forest, the forester selling rights at a daily rate of a few pence for all that could be cut. In 1635 a cutter in Bray reportedly cut sixteen hundred turves a day which he sold for sixpence per hundred (MacDermot 1973, 215).

The forest courts: the Swainmote court

The origins of the Swainmote court are unclear. It is uncertain whether or not a medieval Swainmote court existed on Exmoor, and if it did, precisely what function it held. Thirteenth-century Swainmote courts may have simply been local assemblies called with no purpose in forest law, and no role other than to allow forest wardens a little informal income generation through levying fines against forest inhabitants who failed to attend (Chanter 1907, 282; MacDermot 1973, 74). However, by the 16th century a court known as the Swainmote was certainly in existence, although it bore little relation to the earlier establishment. This was a local court, more resembling a manor court, held before a steward appointed by the warden. It met twice a year in the spring or early summer, the first meeting at Lanacre or Landacre Bridge, and the second opening at Hawkridge Churchyard but closing at Withypool, either at the forest pound or at the inn (Chanter 1907, 282; Siraut 2009, 54–5).

The attendees of this court comprised representatives of two groups, the commoners of those manors bordering the forest, including those in disaforested Devon, known as the 'suitors at large', and of the owners or tenants of the 52 ancient tenements in the parishes of Withypool and Hawkridge, known as the 'free suitors'. The manorial commons, and the archaeological evidence for their use, are discussed in Section 2. The various suitors, however, also held additional rights of common on the royal forest, and it was at least partly in return for these rights that the free suitors and suitors at large 'owed suit' to the Swainmote court. In addition to doing service to the Swainmote, the free suitors helped with the drifts, perambulated the bounds of the forest with the forester every 7 years and, in the unlikely event of a body being found on the forest, served on a coroner's jury of inquest, and in return had additional rights of common of pasture, turbary, estover and piscary (*see* Glossary) on the forest (MacDermot 1973, 184).

A jury comprising 12 suitors was selected at each court, to deal with the minor civil and

Fig 1.3
The meeting place of one of the earliest courts on Exmoor, the Swainmote court, at Landacre Bridge.
[© Rob Wilson-North]

criminal offences, the first against the forest and the second against the 'precincts of the suitors', probably the commons as the Swainmote would not come into conflict with the surrounding manorial courts. No Swainmote court rolls are known to survive but the courts would have dealt with such minor offences as entering the forest with dog, gun or bow, illegal fishing or commoners neglecting their duties at the forest drifts, the 9 yearly drives of the forest to round up all horses, cattle and sheep being pastured there (MacDermot 1973, 208–9; Siraut 2009, 54–5). One of the most important tasks of the Swainmote relating to the pasture of the moor, was to check the stoodirons of the suitors at large, the branding mark used to differentiate their livestock from those of the free suitors, who had right of common on the forest, and those of 'strangers', which were pastured in the forest at full charge; unmarked animals risked being charged full price for pasture or being impounded at the forest pound in Withypool as strays (MacDermot 1973, 190).

By the 16th century royal forest status 'had been largely forgotten' across England (Winchester 2000), and the forest courts became less and less significant. The enforcement of forest law probably ended with the reign of Edward III in the late 14th century. From the 16th century the forest was leased and the deer became the property of the lessee. Exmoor became considered as a 'chase', not a royal forest, and was therefore increasingly governed by common law (MacDermot 1973, 299–300). Nonetheless, the Swainmote court continued to meet into the 19th century, the last being held in 1818, but by this time the business in hand was principally concerned with enjoying the refreshments traditionally provided by the warden, rather than dealing with litigation (Siraut 2009, 55).

Profitable pasture: agistment and crying the moor

The pasture of Exmoor was, arguably, its single greatest resource, and charging for grazing within the royal forest was the primary means of generating income (Winchester 2004, 25). That the area of western Somerset and eastern Devon was well provided with grazing pasture at the end of the 11th century is attested by Domesday Book, even to the extent of 'waste' being laid to grass between 1066 and 1086 – anticipating the 19th-century improvements by almost exactly 800 years (VCH Somerset, parish files). Livestock grazing continued on the moor into the 13th century as the population of Exmoor grew and the Exchequer received a payment of 12s 6d, the value of 14 heifers and a bull paid by the forest commoners to Richard de Plessis (bailiff of the forest). The payment was made to the Crown for the office, on the death of de Plessis in 1289, but the payment by the commoners of such number of livestock would suggest the existence of a sizeable herd (VCH Somerset, parish files; MacDermot 1973, 63).

The greatest income, though, would have been due to de Plessis as he charged the commoners for the agistment or depasturing of livestock on the royal forest. Whether the revenue was collected by the warden or the pasture was sublet to another, known variously as 'the farmer of the agistment' or 'the forester', this was a substantial amount and the main income generated by the forest. The prices charged for agistment were announced by the forester every spring in the market towns around Exmoor, a process known as 'crying the moor'. The number of animals pastured on Exmoor was huge. In addition to the 7,000 or so sheep belonging to the free suitors, for which no charge was made, the forest book of 1736 accounts for nearly 14,000 sheep belonging to the suitors at large and over 16,000 to 'strangers'; many farmers from the neighbouring parishes of north Devon drove their beasts some considerable distance. These numbers are likely to be similar to earlier centuries, and demonstrate the great value and importance of Exmoor's grazing to the hinterland. Cattle and horses were agisted in much lower numbers than sheep, the figures for 1736 being 127 bullocks and 102 colts (MacDermot 1973, 210; Siraut 2009, 88, Fig 51).

The process of agistment involved careful record keeping and a series of checks on incoming and outgoing animals. Before putting their animals onto the moor, each owner advised the forester of his name and parish, his particular mark and the number of sheep, which were duly entered into the 'forest book'. The sheep were pastured in the spring, usually between March and May, where they stayed until shearing time, when they returned to their home farms. It was at this time of transit that the outgoing sheep were counted, or 'told' by tellers appointed by the forester, and any extras were charged double the normal rate.

Nine days before midsummer the forester and the free suitors performed the drift for sheep. By this time most sheep would have been removed for shearing, but any unshorn sheep were rounded up and driven to the forest pound at Withypool, on the south side of the River Barle. The unshorn sheep were sheared, the fleeces by custom going to the forester, and any booked-in sheep then returned to the forest; any others were impounded until mid-summer day, and if unclaimed became the forester's property. Once again being counted on their return other sheep were returned to the forest after shearing, where they stayed until the autumn. The sheep drift was the only one to take place on a regular date every year, the two or thee cattle drifts and five drifts of the moorland horses or ponies taking place at a time of the forester's choosing (MacDermot 1973, 212–4).

Exmoor during the Commonwealth: The decline of the royal forest

In July 1649 the Commonwealth Parliament of England passed 'An Act for the sale of the Honours Manors and Lands heretofore belonging to the late King, Queen and Prince'. Royal forests were specifically excluded from the Act but, as Exmoor was now commonly considered a chase rather than a forest, following a new survey and perambulation of the forest boundary in 1651 the freehold of 'Exmore Chase' was sold in 1652, via an intermediary, to James Boevey, a London merchant of Dutch descent. For the first time in its existence, the forest of Exmoor was now owned by somebody not of royal birth (MacDermot 1973, 299).

Boevey had big plans for Exmoor. He intended to run the chase as a going concern and his business aspirations can be seen in his purchase of the rights to the wool tithes of the forest in 1653. He also had visions of transforming his new acquisition into a country estate and populating the waste with tenanted farms, anticipating Frederic Knight's plans for the moor by 190 years (MacDermot 1973, 321).

He was also probably the first person since prehistoric times to actively enclose, improve and inhabit any land on the forest. In 1654 his new dwelling at Simonsbath, the first house on Exmoor, was complete and by 1670 he claims to have 'improved the Forest by building, manuring and enclosing and otherwise', a statement no doubt relating to the enclosure of 118 acres around the house to create a farm at Simonsbath,

Fig 1.4
By enclosing 48 hectares at Simonsbath James Boevey enclosed the first farm on Exmoor since the creation of the royal forest. The enclosure would have changed little from 1670 to 1818, when this map was made.
[© Somerset Heritage Service Q/RDe 61]

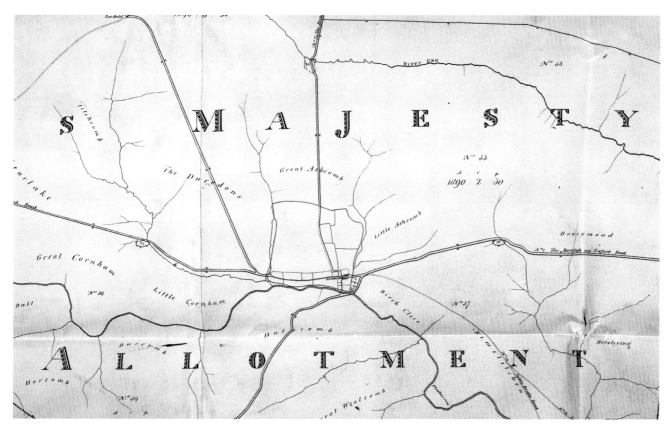

which was farmed by the Hill family from 1657 until at least the 1690s (MacDermot 1973, 223; Siraut 2009, 90; Fig 1.4).

It is probable that the 'otherwise' part of his claims included the creation of a warren. The remains of at least eight pillow mounds or artificial warrens have been identified on the south-facing slopes of the Exe valley, about 2.5km to the north-east of Simonsbath, in front of the much later Warren Farm. Such earthworks are widespread across England but these examples are unusual because they are most likely to date from the 17th century.

Rabbits are not native to Britain. They probably became established following the Norman Conquest and were originally difficult to keep. They did not prosper in damp conditions, such as those prevalent in an Exmoor combe, and much preferred to burrow into slopes of loose and well drained soil. Pillow mounds were therefore built to provide convenient 'pioneer accommodation' and provide shelter to new rabbit colonies in otherwise inhospitable locations, the side ditches acting as drains to keep the burrow dry (Williamson 2007, 53). The expense of creating warrens meant that they were a very valuable and prestigious commodity, kept as much for fur as for meat, and remained so into the 17th century. Rabbits were even exchanged as gifts between landowners (Williamson 2007, 18). New warrens, such as the one in Fig 1.5, were therefore often established in isolated locations and managed by a warrener who lived, at least at times, in a lodge close to the warren. An earthwork platform may indicate the location of such a warrener's hut to the west of this site (Riley and Wilson-North 2001). A warren would certainly fit with Boevey's hardnosed aspirations for his estate, providing food, prestige and possibly income.

Boevey's economic motivation and appreciation of the value of Exmoor's pasture clearly influenced his choice of Simonsbath as the location of his house and as the site for a new forest pound. Simonsbath was a location from which he could easily control and monitor the flow of livestock using the forest. As Robert Pollard of South Molton stated in his deposition of 1654:

> He knows the capital messuage called Symons-bath; it is most convenient for all the borderers and for such as come to enter sheep and cattle and to fetch and drive them away or to pay for the agistments and tythes.
> (MacDermot 1973, 330)

Intent on making a quick return on his investment, Boevey almost doubled the charges for agistment on the forest immediately upon taking possession. However, his assessment of his clients' willingness to pay was somewhat less astute than his choice of location. Many Exmoor farmers continued to pasture their livestock but refused to pay the new rates, while others refused to pasture on the forest altogether, causing Boevey to perform a policy u-turn the following year by slightly reducing his charges. The subsequent agistment charges remained unchanged until John Knight purchased the forest at the beginning of the 19th century. However, incensed at what he saw as impositions on his investment, Boevey began a campaign of litigation against those farmers he saw as responsible for his losses, accusing them of a range of unlikely frauds against him, such as falsely marking their sheep, pasturing them at night and removing them by morning to avoid charges or even the potentially hazardous crime of cutting turf at night. His legal campaigns continued until his death in 1696 (MacDermot 1973, 325, 327–30).

The depositions arising from the litigation do, however, give us an insight into the customs of the forest at this time and how they may have continued to shape the landscape. For example, the statement of Nicholas Slader of North Molton indicates that peat cutting continued on the forest, describing his right to cut turf at a rate of 4d a day. It is ironic, however, that in attempting to argue against the hike in charges the defendants in Boevey's litigation played down the value of the forest grazing. For instance, Slader claimed, 'The land and soyle of Exmore is a vey cold, course and barren soyle, and doth produce a course, mossy and sower grass only serviceable to keep beastes alive, and not to grow and improve them.' Similarly, William Brayley of Swimbridge claims not to have pastured his sheep on the forest for 15 years, 'by reason it was soe course that he could get nothing thereby', and 'such stuffe as doth pasture thereon doe gayne very little thereby, other than for the preservation of their own grounds in the meantime' (MacDermot 1973, 330).

The same depositions may also shed some light on the possible function of some earthworks identified from aerial photographs. For instance, Brayley later refers to the counting or telling (see Glossary) of livestock as they were driven to pasture the forest:

There is a place called 'the Spann' where he did usually drive his sheep in and out of the forest, and there was one appointed at the shearing tyme by the Farmers and Agents to tell sheepe and other cattell, and tooke a note thereof.

(MacDermot 1973, 330)

The telling of livestock as it entered the forest has taken place from the medieval period. William Brayley's evidence suggests that certain places had long been recognised as common access points to the forest. A combination of topography, habit and prudence in avoiding bogs would have determined the route taken to and from the forest, and in the absence of fences or gates, natural 'pinch-points' in the landscape where tracks converge would be the logical place to set-up temporary hurdles to assist in the count (Eardley Wilmot 1990, 25). However, the use of specific buildings, barriers or structures known as

telling houses (*see* Glossary), to monitor the movement of sheep on Exmoor may date from Boevey's time. Hazel Eardley-Wilmot recounts an event recorded as taking place in June 1677, when Boevey's agent happened across an individual by the name of Jennings at Melcombe Hill near Moles Chamber, just outside the forest 'in the King's highway leading from the Forest to South Molton', apparently attempting to pasture his sheep without payment (Eardley-Wilmot 1990, 24). This event, or ones like it, may have been what prompted Boevey to build durable telling houses at key access points into the forest from the surrounding towns and villages, particularly those in north Devon to the south-west of the moor, from where many of the herds originated (Eardley-Wilmot 1990, 25). The existence of such structures has been suggested at several locations close to the forest boundary, including at Span Head on North Molton Common, Moles Chamber and in Hoar Oak valley, with a more

Fig 1.5
On the slopes of Exe Cleave in front of the 19th-century Warren Farm are a series of pillow mounds or artificial rabbit warrens, probably made by James Boevey in the 17th century. The surrounding area is still known as The Warren. [NMR 15306/42 SS7940/7 27-JUN-1995]

Fig 1.6a and b
Tracks converge to enter
the royal forest close to
Alderman's Barrow at the
meeting place of three
parishes, Porlock, Luccombe
and Exford. Near the
trackways low earthworks
may be all that remains of
a telling house. The plan (a)
is based on information
from aerial photographs (b).
[(a) © John Hodgson;
(b) NMR RAF/540/931 (RP)
Frame 3100 08-NOV-1952]

remote example suggested by the name 'Telling House Field' at Yelland Cross, west of Challacombe (c SS 675416) (Burton 1989, 33–4; Eardley-Wilmot 1990, 25–8; MacDermot 1973, 212).

The Span Head telling house was described as a 'rude shelter chiefly constructed of turf', and is now no longer visible, but its remains were remembered when MacDermot (1973, 212) was writing in the early 20th century. Burton was confident that a small circular turf and stone structure he had located on the south side of the old Harepath was the remains of the Moles Chamber telling house, depicted by Day and Masters on their map of 1782 (Burton 1989, 33–4). Burton was also confident telling houses were unlikely to have been built on the Somerset side of the moor, as the sheep from Oare, Porlock and Exford were not pastured on the moor until after shearing (Burton 1989, 43).

The main archaeological evidence for the movement of animals into and across moors is the fragmentary remains of sinuous, braided tracks known as packhorse ways (*see* Case study: Routes across the forest). Recent interpretation of the aerial photographs has revealed a site on the north-eastern side of the royal forest where the boundaries of Porlock and Luccombe parishes converge at Alderman's Barrow. Low earthworks can be seen straddling the spur between the steeply incised combes of Chalk Water and Chetsford Water. The course of the streams effectively prevent access to the forest from parishes to the north and east, including Oare, Porlock and Exford, for some distance to the north and south, and a fan-like array of relict trackways indicate that this ridge has been a natural access point into the forest for many years. The recently discovered earthworks occupy the perfect location to control that access and may indicate the site of a previously unknown telling house.

Upon the restoration of the monarchy in 1660 Exmoor was returned to royal ownership,

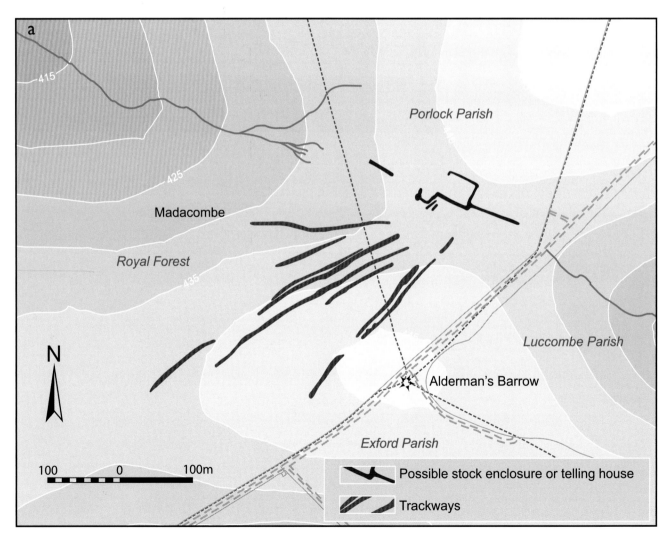

and although the local farmers may have hoped to see Boevey evicted, he retained possession as leaseholder until his death. However, with the exception of the rabbit warren which was later to provide a name for one of the Knights' farms, we have little evidence of any further estate improvement likely to date to Boevey's lifetime. Certainly no new farms were established and it is a little over a century until the next major development in the enclosure of Exmoor.

Enclosure and the beginning of reclamation: the end of the royal forest

All lands are capable of Improvement, none being so profitable by nature as they are capable of being made by man's assistance.
(Hitt 1761, quoted in Tarlow 2007)

In 1819, John Knight, the new owner of the former royal forest of Exmoor, began the construction of a wall 29 miles long around his new estate. It was not a high wall, but its significance was that it physically marked a defining moment in the changing character of Exmoor. The forest of Exmoor had been privately owned since at least the Norman period but to a degree it had always been accessible, exploited for its grazing and other natural resources.

The new forest wall imposed a boundary across this previously open landscape and signified more than just a land purchase; it was a statement, a physical expression of a move away from the historic common rights and forest customs, towards the rights of individual ownership. The wall embodied a range of motivations and aspirations, from the desires of one man to enter into the ranks of landed society, to that society's wider pre-occupation with improving on nature. While the agricultural

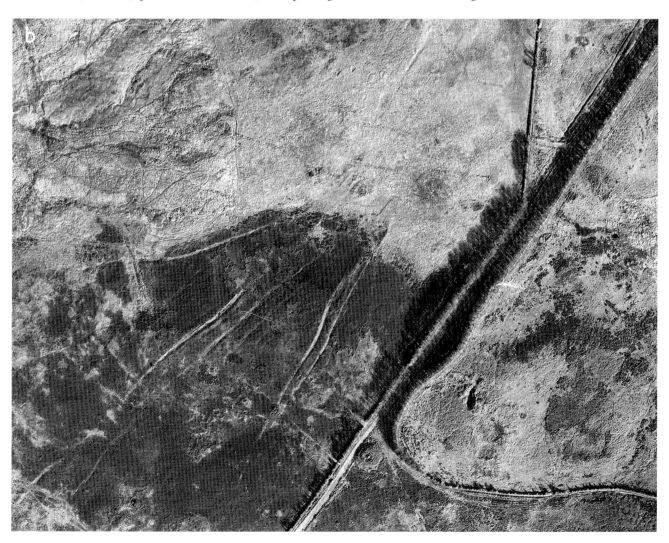

Case study
Routes across the forest

When the forest of Exmoor was enclosed at the beginning of the 19th century there were no roads across it. Instead, a network of informal trackways had developed over centuries, if not millennia. These were used by packhorses and ponies, usually driven in single file, laden with packs and baskets or pulling sledges. Individuals would also have crossed the area on horseback and on foot, while livestock would have been driven on and off the moor at certain times of the year. No vehicle transport was able to cross this difficult and inhospitable landscape until the middle of the 19th century.

The archaeological evidence for these early routeways or packhorse ways is often visible. Sometimes it occurs as a series of roughly parallel, sinuous, braided gulleys. Most frequently these are found on steep valley slopes on either sides of river crossing points. In low sunlight these can be seen at Exe Head, in Squallacombe and near Cornham Ford.

The trackways mark the continual passage of animals across the moor. Over time, the passage of such traffic wore away the ground and the trackways became deep gulleys. When poor weather made the track either treacherous or impassable, a new route was taken alongside the earlier route and the process of eroding a new gulley began again next to the disused one. Over hundreds of years this pattern was repeated again and again, creating sinuous interlaced patterns of gulleys. Aerial photography reveals not only the trackways themselves but also allows them to be perceived as routeways across the landscape.

Sections of these 'ancient' and historic routes have been traced and postulated around and across the forest (Burton 1989; Eardley-Wilmot 1990) but the archaeological evidence incontrovertibly reflects those points that saw the heaviest traffic, such as fords and regular meeting places. The persistence of many of these access points is reflected in their modern names, such as Red Stone Gate, or in association with forest markers, such as at Alderman's Barrow. Given Simonsbath's central role in the forest economy since the 17th century, it is perhaps unsurprising that one of the densest concentrations of trackways can be seen

Fig 1.7a–e
Although many of these routes can be seen on the ground, as at (a) Exe Head, their true extent is best seen from the air, as at (b) Moles Chamber, (c) Squallacombe, (d) Simonsbath, and (e) north of Acklands.
[(a) © Rob Wilson-North; (b) OS/73109 (V) Frame 1039 29-APR-1973 Lib 10456; (c) OS/73087 (V) Frame 621 14-APR-1973 Lib 10455; (d) OS/96507 (V) Frame 31 30-MAR-1996 Lib 15126; (e) OS/96507 (V) Frame 25 30-MAR-1996 Lib 15126]

a

approaching the village from the south, crossing the Barle in the area of Simonsbath Bridge and continuing north-eastwards through what is now Birchcleave Wood.

The local significance of these routes was recognised at enclosure, the Enclosure Award setting out a sequence of numbered roads, depicted on the enclosure map of 1818, 'following, in almost every case, the track-ways already existing' (Orwin and Sellick 1970, 53), and this pattern is recognisable in the transcriptions from aerial photographs. However, there was no obligation to build these roads and many were never made, but the location of several of Exmoor's old inns, such as the Gallon House Inn on the road from Simonsbath to Exford and the Acland Arms near Mole's Chamber, both built after enclosure, reflect the ongoing importance of these local routes (Eardley-Wilmot 1990, 166–7).

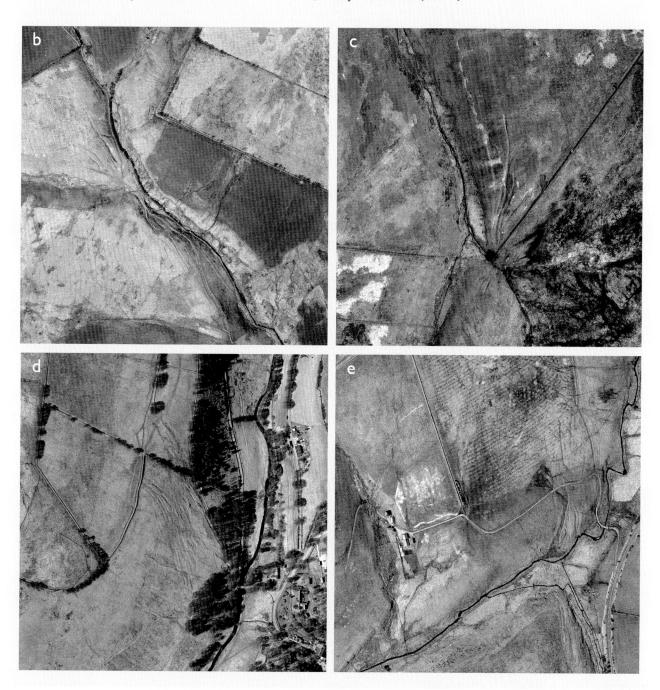

value of the land could be increased, so too could its aesthetic value, as well as the physical and moral improvement of those who lived and worked on it.

Enclosure

Enclosure is a complex subject that is closely linked to the wider question of improvement. Improvement had implications for all walks of life: economic, agricultural, industrial, artistic and even spiritual. It was a national phenomenon but had repercussions far beyond Britain's

shores, as the impact of the industrial and agricultural revolutions reached colonies and plantations in Australia, Africa and the Caribbean. On Exmoor this philosophy is reflected in the historic landscape of 19th-century reclamation. To begin to understand this, we must appreciate the wider attitudes towards enclosure and improvement, and how these may have influenced the Knights' activities on Exmoor.

The terms 'inclosure' and 'enclosure' are often seen as interchangeable. However, there are subtle but important distinctions. Inclosure is the legal term used to describe the process,

Fig 1.8
John Knight's Forest
boundary wall near
Lanacombe.
[© Rob Wilson-North]

by Act of Parliament or agreement, of the consolidation or extension of private landownership over land previously held in common. In contrast, the term enclosure can be used to describe both the act of building hedges or fences to create new fields, and the areas newly enclosed. It is important to make the distinction, as inclosure is not always associated with enclosure, and vice versa (Gillard 2002). Nonetheless, inclosure did often involve enclosure and the loss of any former common rights on the land, albeit often with some degree of compensation, and for the sake of clarity, the latter term will be used for the remainder of the book.

Enclosure is often identified as a precursor of the 'agricultural revolution' of the eighteenth and nineteenth centuries, particularly parliamentary enclosure of the large medieval open-fields of the midland 'champion' regions of England, which resulted in the landscape of rectangular fields and relict ridge and furrow visible today. This is variously argued to be a consequence or driver of the industrial revolution (Williamson 2002).

Enclosure remains a very involved and difficult process to understand. For instance, it is commonly perceived to be an 18th- or 19th-century phenomenon but has in fact taken place, in different ways and for a range of reasons, in different parts of the country from the medieval period onwards (Tarlow 2007, 49). The general absence of open fields in Devon, for example, has been attributed to their 'remarkably early' private enclosure by the early 14th century (Hoskins 1954, 72–3).

As such, it is impossible to generalise about the reasons for enclosure. However, a broad distinction can be drawn between the methods, often called *piecemeal* and *general* enclosure. Piecemeal enclosure resulted in the loss of open fields through a series of private sales or exchanges between landowners, whereby contiguous strips of land were amalgamated into larger holdings, which ultimately were fenced or walled. This was a gradual and irregular process, which often leaves little historic trace. It did not result in dramatic remodelling of field systems but can often still be read in the landscape, for instance, as former strip fields fossilised in the line of later field boundaries (*see* Fig 3.4). Early examples of piecemeal enclosure are known from village clearances of the 14th and 15th centuries (Williamson 2000, 59; 2002, 10).

General enclosure, in contrast, was normally a much larger-scale affair. A single individual could acquire ownership of all land within an area and reorganise and enclose it as they saw fit. Alternatively, if the majority of landowners in an area wanted to enclose open land, they could do so 'by agreement', acting together to consolidate and enclose the available land in one action. Any commons were divided between them in proportion to the rights they previously held over them. This process is characteristic of the 16th to 17th centuries. Although enclosure by agreement continued into the following century, it was soon superseded in the 18th and 19th centuries by parliamentary enclosure, whereby landowners, or those interested in becoming so, as was the case for Exmoor, could petition parliament for an act to enclose. If successful, a board of commissioners caused a survey of the land to be made and subsequently consolidated holdings, awarding parcels of land as compensation to those who had held, and now lost, common rights or interests in the land (Williamson 2000, 59; 2002, 10–11).

This form of enclosure typically resulted in the creation of very regular rectilinear field systems, from first being planned onto enclosure maps and subsequently laid out in the field by surveyors who often ignored even major topographic features to maintain their regularity. This form of enclosure characterises much of the landscape of the midlands, to the extent that Rackham identified this as a zone of 'predominantly planned countryside' (Rackham 1998, Fig 1.3, 4–5), but it can also be seen on a smaller scale around Exmoor, for example, on the former commons of Kentisbury Down to the west of the former royal forest (*see* Section 2, Case study: Parliamentary enclosure of the commons – the holding of Holdstone Down).

Commons were frequently enclosed in this way, but a second type of landscape was often also enclosed by this method, namely areas of previously unenclosed and marginal 'waste', which was seen as ripe for improvement, areas such as the royal forest of Exmoor which was finally enclosed by an Act of Parliament of 1818.

The significance of enclosure for Exmoor

The landscape of irregularly shaped hedged fields, which we can see today, forming the landscape around the former royal forest of Exmoor probably evolved from a system of small fields and closes associated with the surrounding isolated farmsteads and hamlets. Although very different in character from the large open fields that developed in the Midlands, they probably operated on a local variant of open-field cultivation now known as convertible husbandry, which incorporated a significant element of pastoral farming. Unlike the Midlands system, however, convertible husbandry was not reliant on nucleated settlement for communal labour and resources, and instead evolved a compact block of ring-fenced infields around isolated farms, cultivated on long periods of rotation, perhaps of 10 years or more, with short periods of cropping followed by longer periods of grass, possibly 6 to 8 years long. It is likely that no more than one-quarter of the fields within a holding were cultivated in a single year and very little land was laid to permanent pasture within the infield, with rough moorland pasture exploited as an important resource, and even occasionally cultivated (Rippon *et al* 2006). It is probable that convertible husbandry continued to be practised until at least the 16th century and despite farm abandonment and amalgamation in the post-

medieval period, many infield boundaries have proved to be durable features within the landscape (Riley and Wilson-North 2001, 125–8). Nevertheless, although this landscape did not create the wide open spaces suited to large-scale general enclosure as in the Midlands, where parliamentary enclosure would account for almost half of the enclosed lands, the infields of ancient enclosure were more susceptible to processes of piecemeal enclosure and enclosure by agreement.

In contrast, areas of common grazing, such as the neighbouring royal forest of Exmoor, often remained unenclosed until parliamentary enclosure. Thus Exmoor remained one of the last great wastes in England, and, excluding Bodmin, the last in the south-west, Dartmoor having already been subject to improvement. Although undoubtedly important to the local economy, Exmoor's unenclosed moorlands would have been perceived by the improving mindset as an inefficient use of land, presenting an irresistible challenge and opportunity for parliamentary enclosure.

Fig 1.9
The regularly planned and rectilinear fields of parliamentary enclosure on Kentisbury Down on the west side of Exmoor. In the far distance, the rounded profile of Holdstone Down – one of the last areas of England to be subject to the process of enclosure – overlooks the Bristol Channel. [NMR 26643/037 (UNCAT) 18-AUG-2009]

Why was Exmoor enclosed? A prelude to improvement

As the expiry of his lease approached in 1814, Sir Thomas Acland, 10th Baronet and last warden of Exmoor forest, approached the Commissioners of His Majesty's Woods, Forests and Land Revenues with a proposal to buy the leasehold of the forest. His move was ultimately unsuccessful but was the catalyst that began the process of enclosure, a process which culminated in the sale in 1818 of the forest at auction to John Knight, a Worcestershire ironmaster, for the sum of £50,000 (Orwin and Sellick 1970).

But what prompted Sir Thomas Acland to propose such a dramatic move after 200 years of Acland family stewardship? And what drove a Midlands industrialist, with little knowledge of Exmoor, to invest a considerable fortune into the purchase of a vast waste some distance from his home and equally far from his experience in ironworking, which would surely offer a safer and more profitable investment?

The answer to both of these questions can be called a desire for improvement. Improvement is a label that has been used to describe a multitude of motivations: economic historians refer to improvement in terms of 18th- and 19th-century rural land management aimed at improving agricultural productivity and efficiency, while landscape historians focus on the aesthetic aspects of estate management, for instance, the creation of deer parks, landscaping or vistas. Although encompassing both elements, the ideology of improvement was broader than either of these alone, and the 18th- and 19th-century elite applied the term to almost any aspect of life, agricultural and economic, aesthetic and moral (Tarlow 2007, 34).

However, agricultural improvement became a primary concern for landowners. The rise of 'scientific farming' after 1750 was no doubt influenced in part by George III, known as 'Farmer George' due to his passion for agriculture, which went so far as to incorporate the cultivation of oats and barley into the gardens at Kew and conducting experiments to improve British sheep breeds, pasturing his flocks on the lawns at Richmond.

Other factors were important, however. Whereas Farmer George epitomised the mid-18th-century gentleman farmer, promoting reform on his own land, by the late 18th century the expansion of agriculture was encouraged by the Napoleonic Wars and the patriotic drive to extend cultivation to its limits, encouraged of course by the concomitant high price of corn. State support was also extended in the form of parliamentary enclosure and state-sponsored assessments of the 'general view' of agriculture in each county. For instance, Billingsley's prescient assessment of Exmoor in the Somerset 'general view' of 1794 reads:

A very large proportion of the whole needs but the spirit and fortune of some one or more of our wealthy Gentlemen of England, whose attention, if turned this way, sanctioned by the Royal proprietor, would render the Forest of Exmoor in a few years as fair a prospect as the surrounding country, and not a useless and void space in the map of the county of Somerset. Excepting for a few willows and thorns by the side of the rivulets, not a tree or a bush is to be seen on the whole forest, but plantations of most kinds need no more shelter nor better soil than is met with here. Let there be a small town or village erected near the middle, suppose by Simonsbath, which should form proper residences for articifers and husbandmen employed in building farmhouses and enclosing many a considerable estate around them.

(Billingsley 1794, 43–4)

It has been suggested that by the mid-19th century very few traditional farmers were left in the country, as only using those methods developed by scientific farming would permit further improvement on already reclaimed ground (Tarlow 2007, 36–7). The proliferation of new agricultural societies, including the Royal Agricultural Society of England (founded 1838, motto 'Practice with Science') and their resultant journals, plus swathes of other publications such as Henry Stephens' (1854) *The Book of the Farm*, first published in 1844, espousing the latest technological innovations, inventions and practices to assist the new scientific farmer, would go some way to support this idea. The improvement movement's imperatives of efficiency and a moral duty to reduce waste even filtered into the domestic sphere with popular publications, such as Mrs Beeton's (1861) *Book of Household Management*.

Agricultural improvement, however, was considered impossible without enclosure. The new farming methods and scientific techniques were interconnected, and often inseparable. For instance, the implementation of new crop rotations may need soil improvement, extensive drainage or the use of new equipment, such as steam-powered ploughs, all of which were almost impossible to implement individually or across the small mixed holdings of common fields. In addition, the newest scientific farming methods were also expensive, and therefore the capital costs of large reclamation and improvement schemes were beyond the means of all but the most wealthy of landowners. However, although enclosure, and therefore improvement, was intrinsically connected to the development of capitalism (Williamson 2000, 57), making money was not necessarily the primary driver:

> Improvement had a moral value and a social desirability far beyond the mere enhancement of profit, and it is easy to find numerous examples of landowners who spent vastly more money on enclosing, draining, fertilising and clearing than they were ever able to recover in increased rents.
> (Tarlow 2007, 35)

Following the end of the Napoleonic Wars, Britain's population increased dramatically, doubling between 1800 and 1850 (Williamson 2002, 6). Whether agricultural improvement was a reaction to the need to feed an increasingly industrialised and urbanised society, or whether the population increase and industrialisation was facilitated by increased agricultural productivity is a much debated point (Overton 1996; Tarlow 2007). What is perhaps more relevant here is that people believed improvement, and agricultural expansion, was necessary. As Robert Smith, the agent for Frederic Knight for many years stated in 1856:

> The reclaiming of moorlands deserves attention among other improvements of our native agriculture as one means of providing food for an increasing population.
> (Smith 1856, 349)

By the 19th century the best agricultural land had long been enclosed. Therefore, as Robert Smith's statement implies, previously marginal land was being increasingly contemplated by the aspiring improver, land which by definition needed the most improvement. The impressions of Exmoor given by 18th- and 19th-century writers are frequently uncomplimentary. Arguably the best known is that of Daniel Defoe, quoting the earlier writings of Camden following his journeys around Britain between 1724 and 1727:

> Leaving the coast, we came, in our going southward, to the great river Ex, or Isca, which rises in the hills on this north side of the county, and that so far, as, like the Tamar, it begins within four or five miles of the Severn Sea; the country it rises in, is called Exmore, Cambden calls it a filthy, barren, ground, and, indeed, so it is …
> (Defoe, 1927, 263)

Nonetheless, it would appear that by the time of the 1814 report by the Commissioners for Enclosure, 'local opinion' was in favour. Indeed, enclosure at the end of Acland's lease was not only expected but was positively anticipated as a 'prelude to improvement' (Orwin and Sellick 1970).

John Knight and Exmoor

Although John Knight's fortune was made in the iron industry, the Knights were a very influential family in late 18th- and early 19th-century society and, although not aristocracy, close relatives were at the forefront of the Georgian aesthetic improvement movement. His father was cousin to Richard Payne Knight, whose predecessors invested their industrial wealth in land, allowing Payne Knight to indulge in the arts and to develop the family seat, Downton Castle near Ludlow in Herefordshire, into a castellated mansion and become one of the foremost proponents of the picturesque movement (Caroline Garrett, pers comm). In addition, Elizabeth Knight, cousin of Richard Payne Knight, married into the Johnes family of Hafod Uchtryd, near Aberystwyth, a vast wild estate that was crafted by Thomas Johnes to become a landscape of savage and 'natural' picturesque beauty (Garrett 2004). Significantly, Johnes was also a passionate social and agricultural improver, building farms and cottages, planting woodlands and experimenting with livestock breeds and cultivating new crops. Unfortunately his experiment ended in bankruptcy and tragedy (Garrett 2004; National Library of Wales Welsh Biography online http://wbo.llgc.org.uk). Somewhat closer to Exmoor, John Knight's sister, Mary, married Coplestone Warre Bampfylde, who developed extensive and famous gardens at his house at Hestercombe, near Taunton (Garrett 2004; Orwin and Sellick 1970, 27–31).

The development of estates already in existence around Exmoor would also have been well known to John Knight. Thomas Dyke Acland, the 10th Baronet, built farms and cottages at their estates at Holnicote, Pixton and the Devon family seat at Killerton. He also employed John Veitch, founder of the famous Veitch nurseries, to oversee tree planting at Killerton and Holnicote (Isabel Richardson, pers comm). Veitch was also commissioned in 1792 to landscape the Deer Park at Nettlecombe, the principle seat of the Trevelyan family, in the fashion of Lancelot 'Capability' Brown, an embellishment that included the clearance of a settlement on the southern edge of the park. The residents were rehoused at Woodford, but as the cottages here are dated 1824, 1852 and 1865 it would appear this was a long process (Riley and Wilson-North 2001, 135; Rose and Wolseley 1984, 126). Likewise the Luttrell's 18th-century remodelling of Dunster Castle, with a deer park, a bowling green atop the medieval motte and the extravagant Conygar tower were well established by the time Knight purchased the forest (Riley and Wilson-North 2001, 135).

The potential for the improvement of Exmoor may even have been highlighted by events on Dartmoor, which had previously been maligned at least as badly as Exmoor, being described by John Laskey in 1795 as 'the fag end of natures work' (Gregory 2008).

Moves to bring parliamentary enclosure to Dartmoor were mooted in the 1790s but received little support, owing in part to the thorny issue of resolving common rights. As a consequence the improvement of Dartmoor was limited to a number of smaller estates, which became established in the decades after 1780, often evolving from the expansion of the ancient tenements around the former forest. Although not achieving the impact of the Knights' efforts on Exmoor, the most notable of these, and perhaps synonymous with the late 18th- and early 19th-century improvement of Dartmoor, was that of Thomas Tyrwhitt. As Gregory (2008, 213) states:

It was the new estates, created on a large scale, often on virgin sites and generally by 'outsiders' which were to have the greatest effect on the moorland landscape – both in terms of its visual appearance of the area and in the way people perceived it.

The reclamations of Tyrwhitt and his contemporaries, most particularly their establishment of new towns (Tyrwhitt's new mansion at Tor Royal formed the nucleus of the settlement that was to become Princetown), began to change wider perceptions of the waste, rehabilitating them into places to be developed, not avoided, and most pertinent here, as places suitable for a gentleman to create his estate (Gregory 2008).

John Knight was probably aware of Tyrwhitt's Dartmoor reclamations, and the trajectory of his tale clearly has several striking parallels with that of Exmoor. Tyrwhitt selected a central location at Tor Royal for his mansion, and elements of his settlement suggest that he perceived it at least to some extent aesthetically as well as practically. Facing economic pressures similar to those later faced by the Knights, Tyrwhitt also initiated ambitious but ultimately unsuccessful diversification schemes, including a railway to transport granite from Princetown to Plymouth. Nonetheless, by the time of Vancouver's *General View of the Agriculture of Devon* in 1808, little ground had been made on the improvement of Dartmoor, and by the time John Knight was beginning his Exmoor venture, even Tyrwhitt's reclamations were coming under sceptical scrutiny. By the 1820s Tyrwhitt's improvements were returning to nature and he sold his estate in 1829 (Gregory 2008).

Nonetheless, given this vibrant and entrepreneurial atmosphere of improvement, it was hardly surprising that when the increasingly rare opportunity arose to acquire an entire upland landscape, John Knight eagerly, if unknowingly, bid a sum 10 times greater than the last forest warden, and £20,000 higher than his nearest rival, Earl Fortescue (Orwin and Sellick 1970). As the local press reported in 1818:

Mr Knight of Worcestershire has purchased the allotment (10,000 acres) given in right to the Crown, on Exmoor Forest, for £50,000. The property is near Simonds-Bath; and the greater part is to be inclosed by a wall, in the centre of which a handsome residence is to be built. The spot affords great facilities for this purpose, and will under the judicious plans in contemplation become an enviable possession.
(Local press, August 1818, quoted in Orwin and Sellick 1970, 43)

With the second award of the Commissioners for Enclosure in 1818, the royal forest of Exmoor ceased to exist, and in the following year, the reclamation of the Exmoor estate began.

Draining the moors

The Hill-top and other rough land should be set out ... as summering ground for young cattle, store sheep, colts, ponies &c ... to be subsequently improved by 'surface drainage', similar to the Scotch plan of 'sheep-drains' – an inexpensive process, yet found of infinite value.

(Smith 1856, 355)

So wrote Robert Smith in his prize-winning essay published in the *Journal of the Royal Agricultural Society of England (JRASE)*, on 'Bringing moorland into cultivation', published after 37 years of reclamation by the Knight family on Exmoor.

The primary aim for many large-scale reclamations, including John Knight's plans for Exmoor, was arable cultivation, or at the very least mixed farming on the sheep–corn model. This is reflected, for instance, in Tyrwhitt's plans for Dartmoor, where he aimed 'to reclaim and clothe with grain and grasses' (Gregory 2008).

In the reclamation of Exmoor the raising of stock was originally perceived only as part of a wider system of hill-farming. However, before the futility of attempting large-scale arable farming on Exmoor's peatlands was fully appreciated, and it was recognised that subsoiling was the only effective method of draining these waterlogged soils, surface drains were seen as a vital first step in reclaiming the moorland for cultivation and improved pasture. Such drains are often referred to as 'Scottish' or 'Scotch' sheep-drains due to their use in improving sheep-pasture north of the border. They were prevalent in the borders region but were also

encouraged as far north as the Highlands. For example, in Sutherland, perhaps most infamous for controversial highland clearances, the local press reported in 1821:

We learn that in the county of Sutherland there are some farms, on each of which, within the last five or six years, upwards of 50 miles of sheep drains have been executed.

(Barron 1903, 193)

In this instance, Exmoor's association with Scotland and Sutherland in particular is a tenuous one, but the reclamation of Exmoor had a more direct relationship with the Sutherland estate in the 1870s. Nonetheless, it is certain that John Knight initiated several large-scale drainage schemes on the sheep-drain model. Burton states that in 1836 men were employed to cut such drains: 628 chains (7¾ miles [12.5km]; a chain is 66 feet, one-eighteenth of a mile) of 'Floting Gutters' at Ashcombe, 'which were ... a complete success', and 2,741 perches (8½ miles [13.74km]; a perch varied in length from 16.5 to 24 feet) of surface drains on the Chains, with more at Blackpitts, both of which were apparently failures (Burton 1989, 72). It may be that Burton misinterpreted the reference to 'Floting Gutters' at Ashcombe, as the term 'floting' (floating) is more often used to refer to the creation of irrigation systems known as 'catch meadows' than drains, a farm-scale improvement which also was a vital part of the reclamation of Exmoor, and which will be discussed in more detail in Section 3.

That the Knights had cut drains on the moors has been known for many years. In 1929 Orwin

Fig 1.10
Shallow drains on Lanacombe.
[© Rob Wilson-North]

stated that John Knight, and more particularly his son, cut miles of drains at Great and Little Buscombe, Trout Hill, East and West Pinford and the Chains, and that:

> although they failed completely in their purpose, they remain to this day, to the discomfiture of the unwary stag-hunter who attempts to cross them.
>
> (Orwin and Sellick 1970, 56)

Writing in 1911, MacDermot's views of the Exmoor landscape possibly reflect the ambiguous way in which the 19th-century improvements were viewed with hindsight:

> [Exmoor] was in the same state in the year 800 as in 1800, and as regards a large portion of it, in 1900, save for a few fences and drainage gutters.
>
> (MacDermot 1973, 4)

More recently, in relation to the drainage on the Chains, Burton stated that 'they were of no benefit whatever, and have on more than one occasion since caused the downfall of unwary horsemen and walkers' (Burton 1989, 72).

Despite these later negative views, the sheep-drains were seen by contemporary improvers as an important tool. The NMP survey of Exmoor has used aerial photographs to confirm that sheep-drains were indeed cut across the moors, but has also revealed for the first time the staggering scale of this exercise and the detailed configuration of the systems. In excess of 200km of drains have been recorded within the former royal forest.

If we look at one of these areas, drained towards the end of what has been called the 'demesne farming' phase of the Knights' reclamation of Exmoor, we can perhaps see hints of the development of the practice over time (Orwin and Sellick 1970, 57–72). On the

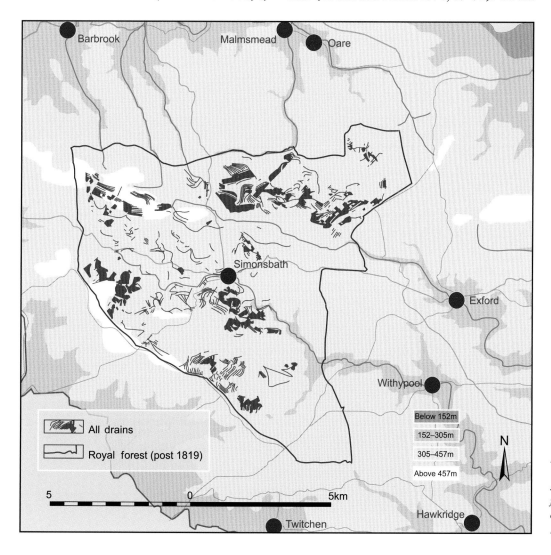

Fig 1.11
The extent of the drainage schemes across Exmoor forest as mapped from aerial photographs.
[© John Hodgson]

Chains, for instance, where 'Richard Bale cut 2,741 perches [8 ½ miles] of surface drains, for which he received £8. 11. 5' (Burton 1989, 72), we can see several individual and fairly discrete areas of drainage. In fact aerial survey has revealed that on the Chains alone, around 25km of drains had been cut, although it is unlikely that Richard Bale was responsible for cutting all of it. Indeed, variation in the style of drainage of the Chains indicates at least two and probably many more phases of draining. For instance, to the south of Hoaroak Water and the Chains Valley are several curvilinear and roughly parallel channels, which closely follow the contours of the hill. In contrast, to the north of Driver Farm and around Pinkery Pond straighter drains cut obliquely across the contours of the slope, whereas near the Chains Valley a third type can be seen crossing, or being crossed by, one of the groups of contour drains at roughly 90 degrees to the slope. These drains may at first glance appear to be randomly located, but closer consideration reveals that the drains clearly relate to the enclosure landscape. The seemingly arbitrarily grouped

drains are contained within, separated by or even actively follow the line of the enclosure fences. Similar patterns of landscape-scale relationships can be seen elsewhere, such as on Great Woolcombe or Lanacombe, where similar but even larger and more complex drainage systems clearly respect the fences or other manmade features such as sheepfolds, indicating some time depth to this process.

Probably the most extensive area of drainage recorded on aerial photographs by the NMP can be seen covering an area of over 240 hectares of steep hill and combe-side between Trout Hill and Brendon Two Gates. This massive drainage scheme, centred on Lanacombe, is a testament to the Knights' commitment to reclaiming Exmoor and the belief in drainage as the cornerstone of their enterprise. Although extensive in coverage, the individual drains are quite small in size, individually measuring up to 1.2m in width and rarely more than 0.5m deep.

As usual the drains are cut in blocks of roughly parallel channels. However, the arrangement of the drains here is much more complex than elsewhere. There is a clear division

Fig 1.12a and b
Detailed layout of drainage systems across the Chains.
[(a) © John Hodgson;
(b) AP OS/73109 (V)]
Frame 927 29-APR-1973
Lib 10456]

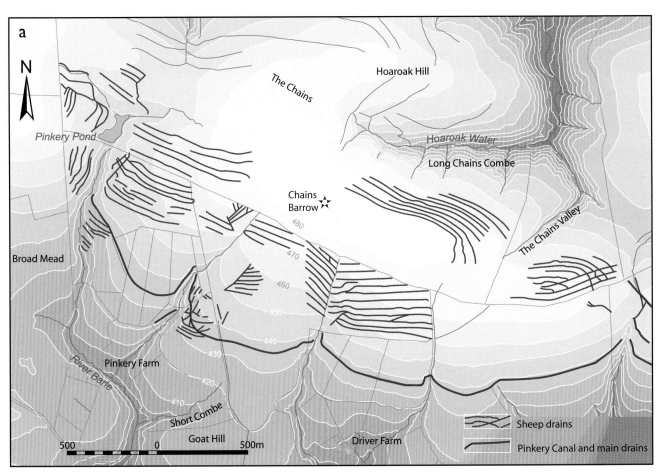

between straight and curvilinear drains even within the same group, and greater variation in the spacing between drains: the majority are 10–50m apart, but some are separated by distances of nearly 100m.

A feature seen nowhere else on Exmoor is the cutting of cross-drains on the south-facing slopes of Little Buscombe overlooking the River Exe. This alone would indicate that at least two phases of drainage took place. The shorter and straighter drains may form the earlier phase, extending eastwards past the current line of the Trout Hill Fence, but possibly within an area enclosed by an earlier line of the boundary, which can be seen to dogleg at its southern end. A later phase of enclosure perhaps realigned this boundary to its current course, heading south over the River Exe, with the second phase of curvilinear cross drains abutting the new line of the enclosure fence, possibly post-dating the expansion of enclosure that accompanied Frederic Knight's creation of tenanted farms in the 1840s and 1850s. That there was a later phase of surface drainage may be indicated elsewhere, for instance in the way that similar

drains appear to respect the sites of two square sheepfolds on Great Woolcombe, which themselves could date to the 1870s.

One clear difference between here and the Chains is the absence of small contour gutters. Whether straight or curved, the drains cross the contours with the clear intent of transporting collected water to be drained into the surrounding spring-fed streams and tributaries. Spring water when percolating naturally to the surface through moorland vegetation was seen as undesirable and detrimental to the growth of any pasture below it (Smith 1856). In contrast, if it could be intercepted before emerging at a spring-head, the water was a good resource and may be beneficially transported by drains for use elsewhere, perhaps to improve the pasture via a catch meadow.

The exception to this rule is an enigmatic embanked channel following the 425m contour roughly east to west which, along its length, has been used to define the edge of enclosure between Blackpitts and Warren Farm. Similar in scale to Pinkery Canal to the south, it may be of the same date, although

b

there are problems in interpreting it. Unlike the Pinkery Canal, however, it does appear to have a relationship with sheep-drains, particularly the area of cross-drains immediately to the north. Such intensive drainage could simply reflect an area of unusually boggy ground, but alternatively could reflect a desire to prevent the run-off of poor-quality water spoiling the enclosed and improved pasture of Prayway Meads below. That the cross-drains appear to feed directly into the large contour-gutter could also indicate that a primary function of this channel was water management related to reclamation and improvement. However, as with Pinkery Canal, this channel does not appear to be designed to transport the water away from the site by gravity, and this does not preclude that a further, as yet undiscovered purpose may exist.

Surprisingly, one detail which remains a mystery is precisely how such drains were cut. Until now it has been assumed that such extensive systems must have been made with mechanical assistance, possibly even associated with Frederic Knight's experiment with steam-powered reclamation (see below). Although steam ploughing and subsoiling was effective in draining the waterlogged and peaty soils on Exmoor, it was a

method best suited to level ground and regularly shaped fields and was a method which could only really operate in straight lines (J Brown, pers comm). It is clear that the topography of the moors and the appearance of the drains, many of which are curving, do not fit these criteria, and they are therefore unlikely to have been created by machine. In fact it is likely that each drain created by the Knights was cut by hand making this an even more extraordinary achievement.

Steam subsoiling was very effective on Exmoor, and was often employed once the surface had been drained. Subsoiling proved to be the only method of breaking the impervious subsurface ironpan, allowing the soil to drain. After this the ground could be successfully cultivated to such a degree that little evidence of the subsoiling process is left visible. The evidence could therefore be read to say that visible drains are in fact, as claimed by Orwin and Sellick, Burton and MacDermot, an indicator of failed (or abandoned) improvement.

There were earlier attempts at subsoiling on Exmoor, carried out with a plough and a team of six bullocks or oxen, but there is no evidence this was the method used to cut the sheep-drains (MacDermot 1973, 4).

Fig 1.13 (below)
Detailed mapping of the surface drains on and around Lanacombe from information on aerial photographs.
[© John Hodgson]

Fig 1.14 (facing page)
An aerial photograph of Lanacombe showing the patterns of drains (the rectangular enclosure is the sheepfold known as Buscombe Beeches).
[OS/73109 (V) Frame 868 29-APR-1973 Lib 10456]

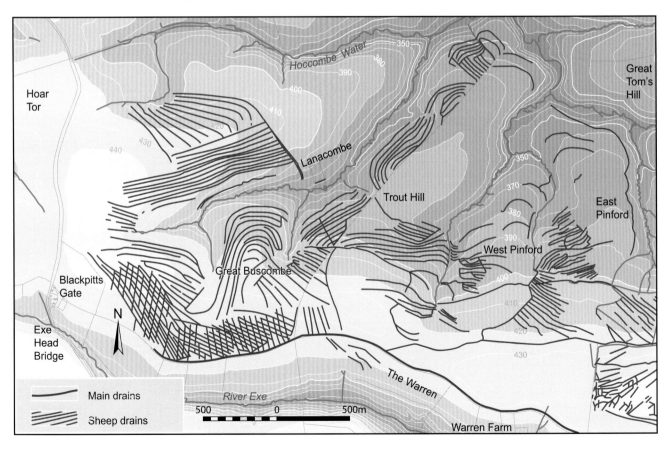

In 1840 John Knight suffered a massive financial setback when he failed to inherit the Downton estate as expected. As a consequence, less money was available for his Exmoor experiment. During the following decade Frederic Knight came to realise that his father's great vision was unviable. Although under his management the estate developed along different lines – that of tenanted farmsteads – he initially continued to pursue the improvers' ideal of cultivating the reclaimed moorland (Orwin and Sellick 1970). Drainage remained central to this task and, almost a decade after his appointment, Robert Smith was still of the view that 'The first operation in the cultivation of an un-improved hill-farm is that of draining' (Smith, 1856, 370).

Robert Smith was appointed as the estate's resident agent in 1848, some seven years after John Knight passed the management to his son Frederic. Smith's 1856 essay reflects not only the continuing obsession with reclaiming and improving marginal lands, but also the view that much of the arable land in 'more favourable altitudes' had already been reclaimed and that 'the great work of reclaiming the 'real moors' yet remains to be done' (Smith, 1856, 351).

The perceived value of drainage was evident in its inclusion as the first 'durable improvement' to be explicitly provided for in the generous leases offered to the tenants of the new Exmoor farmsteads. Smith is credited with introducing leases on what was known as 'the Lincolnshire principle' to the south-west, in which the landlord provided basics such as farm buildings and enclosing the holding, but tenants were responsible for making much of the subsequent improvements upon their farms including drainage, liming and further fencing. The tenant's outlay was offset by initially very low rents and a degree of compensation in the event of their quitting the farm before they had the opportunity to reap the benefits of their improvements (Orwin and Sellick 1970, 78, 87–92).

For example, a copy of a memorandum reproduced in 1856, states:

1st. If the tenant drains the land at his own expense, with the consent and subject to the inspection of the landlord or his agent, an allowance to be made for the materials and workmanship, for [eight to fourteen years as the case may be] years, so that the allowance shall yearly diminish in equal proportions, and be cancelled by years' enjoyment of the improvement.

(Smith 1856, 368)

Case study
Peat cutting in the forest – Blackpitts and the Chains

By 1836 Simonsbath had become the centre of the Knights' Exmoor estate and the demand for fuel within the previously unpopulated former royal forest increased. As Burton says:

> With a great expansion in the population of Simonsbath a great expansion in the production of peat for fuel took place, and by September, 129,500 turves had been cut and dried at Blackpitts, 117,500 of them by Richard Wilkey who at 4s. a thousand was paid £23. 10. 0 for his labours.
>
> (1989, 72)

Long before the first shepherds' huts were built, Blackpitts had derived its evocative name from the peat cutting that had been carried out there since at least the medieval period. Under royal ownership the amount of peat cut within the forest was potentially limited by two factors: the level of the neighbouring population and the number of those willing to pay to the forest warden 4d a day for the privilege, when many had rights to cut turf on the commons. Of course some tried to take peat without payment. In 1270 the court of Eyre in Ilchester fined several residents of Withypool for making turbaries 'in the demesne of the Lord King without warrant' (MacDermot 1973, 90). During the interregnum Boevey increased the daily rate for peat cutting from 6d to 1s 6d and following his death it is likely that the system changed, the rights to cut peat on the former royal forest sold singly to the highest bidder (Burton 1989, 53).

There is extensive evidence for 19th-century peat cutting around Blackpitts. Shallow cuttings are difficult to see on the ground, visible often only as changes in vegetation. The pits resolve into patterns from the air and the NMP survey has recorded over 136 hectares of peat cuttings on the hilltops of Dure Down, Exe Plain, Hoar Tor and Little Buscombe. Some of the smaller and irregular cuttings, such as those visible on Dure Down to the south of Blackpitts may be sporadic and ad hoc cutting. A small patch of pits adjacent to Blackpitts cottage may have provided fuel to the shepherds who bided there.

Fig 1.15 (right)
An enormous turf stack in the garden of a Simonsbath cottage illustrates the scale of late 19th-century peat cutting by local residents. [Courtesy of Sante Lafuenti]

Fig 1.16 (below)
Small and irregular peat cuttings on Dure Down to the south of Blackpitts. [RAF/CPE/UK/1980 (RP) Frame 3154 11-APR-1947 Lib 585]

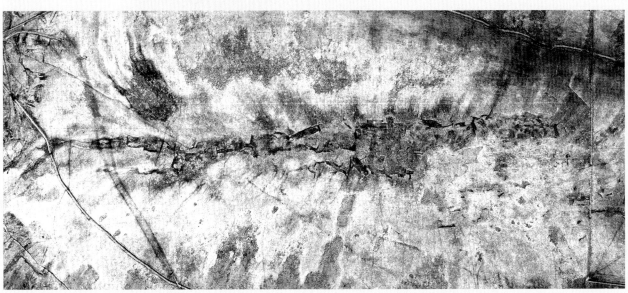

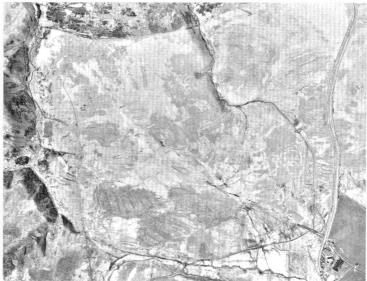

However, much of the evidence is large rectilinear pits, some over 200m long and 40m wide. Pits this size could only have been formed by repeated and regular extraction. It is likely that much of this dates to the Knights' tenure on Exmoor. Nevertheless, peat cutting is a destructive process and successive cutting would erase any evidence of earlier workings, so traces of peat cutting dating back to the medieval period may not necessarily survive.

On Exmoor peat had always primarily been a domestic fuel, whereas on both Bodmin and Dartmoor peat had long been used in industrial processes, such as tin smelting (Herring *et al* 2008). Small-scale peat cutting continued on the Chains under the Knights and probably later, indicated by extraction pits which cleverly used the cuttings of the earlier, failed, sheep-drains to access the peat. In the early 20th century the 4th Earl Fortescue, then owner of the Exmoor estate, perhaps recognising the wider economic potential of this resource, developed plans to industrialise peat cutting on the Chains. In 1910 he entered into talks with the International Carbonising Company, who used a 'wet carbonising process' to artificially transform peat into a more efficient fuel known as 'peat coal'. Negotiations dragged on until 1914, even including surveying a railway route across the Chains to carry the peat-coal and other produce from the moor, but these plans were never realised (Burton 1989, 172).

Fig 1.17 (top left)
A small area of peat cutting pits close to Blackpitts.
[OS/95026 (V) Frame 072 12-MAR-1995 Lib 14644]

Fig 1.18 (above)
Large peat cutting pits.
[ENPA MAL 13/77 113–114 20-MAY-1977]

Fig 1.19 (left)
Small-scale peat cuttings on the Chains. Some of the workings have taken advantage of the cuttings of the earlier sheep drains.
[OS/73109 (V) Frame 927 29-APR-1973 Lib 10456]

Such leases were developed in arable farming and not hill-farming regions, which may partly account for how unprepared many of the early tenants on the former royal forest were for the scale of outlay required to tame their new holdings. Those who did not get cold feet at the outset, often had very short stays. Nonetheless, to the new improvers these leases were a step forward. In describing the farming of Somerset in 1851, Thomas Dyke Acland repeats the motto of 'a distinguished farmer' as 'Liberal leases and grateful tenants' (Acland and Sturge 1851, 7).

We can be also be certain that at least some of the more persistent or progressive tenants did cut such drains on their holdings. In his essay of 1856 Robert Smith describes the challenges that hill farmers face in draining the land and some of the options open to them. Comparing the archaeological evidence of the drainage schemes on aerial photographs with those depicted in his representation of Emmett's Grange (*see also* Case study: Emmett's Grange), although somewhat stylised, we could hazard an interpretation that the evidence represents

Fig 1.20
'Occasional spring' drains between Simonsbath and Little Ashcombe. Compare with Fig 1.26 taken nearly 50 years earlier.
[OS/95026 (V) Frame 105 12-MAR-1995 Lib 14644]

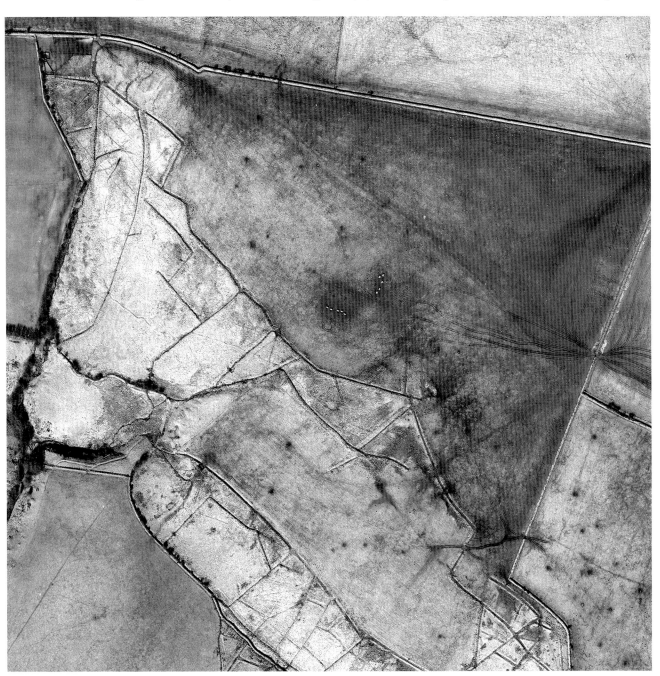

Smith's approach to the problem of impervious 'strata' such as 'tight rock or clay' causing surface water to emerge from a hillside as undesirable springs rendering the ground 'moist and swampy' or 'poisoning all the ground below them'. In such an instance the recommended action included cutting 'a deep "open drain" from bottom to top of the valley', and 'to tap all springs that remain at the sides or otherwise, and so conduct them as to empty into the permanent open drain' (Smith 1856, 371).

In contrast, a smaller but more complex system of drains to the north, between Simonsbath and Little Ashcombe may be a response to 'occasional springs' on moderately sloped lands, for which:

> it may be best to check their descent by making horizontal drains of some length across the declivities of the hills, and thus conduct or empty them into the nearest brooks or open ditches. But should these horizontal drains run in line with the strata or strike on the country, it will be necessary to keep them a little below the porous stratum that supplies the water and cause occasional *upright* drains to be driven across them; by this means the upper line of water issuing from behind some impervious bed or rock will be effectually tapped and cured.
>
> (Smith 1856, 373)

Of course, both of these descriptions could be applied to the enormous contour gutters of Lanacombe and Pinkery Canal – for that is what they seem to be – illustrating that there is still a considerable way to go before the Knight enterprise is fully understood.

Scotland, sheep and stells: the sheep ranching experiment

John Knight's enthusiasm for improvement is illustrated by his journeys around Britain, collecting both inspiration and materials for his Exmoor experiment. During his travels to Scotland in 1826 he admired the Duke of Portland's heathland reclamations near Carlisle and viewed a water meadow near Edinburgh, which might have inspired similar works on Exmoor. Such journeys also stimulated his attempts at developing Exmoor's livestock, introducing West Highland and Hereford Cattle, Cheviot sheep and improving Exmoor ponies by cross-

breeding with thoroughbred stallions (Orwin and Sellick 1970, 62–3).

Perhaps he was also mindful of the fact that since the medieval period sheep had provided the wardens of Exmoor with much of their income, and although the practice of agistment lessened with enclosure he retained a flock of Exmoor Horn sheep for grazing and to eat the root crops in the four-course rotation system he persevered with, long after it was clearly failing. He attempted to improve his flock for wool and meat, by breeding with imported Cheviots and even Merino sheep, but the new and improved stock either proved to be too difficult to manage or too feeble to survive the harsh Exmoor winters (Orwin and Sellick 1970, 65–6).

For the single shepherds employed to run John Knight's herdings, the extreme isolation of Exmoor also made it a lonely and lawless place. Retaining staff proved difficult (Orwin and Sellick 1970). Ultimately John Knight's experiments in improvement proved 'disappointing and inconclusive' (Burton 1989, 112), but with better infrastructure and management, sheep farming was to prove the salvation of the estate. Frederic Knight took control of the estate in 1841 and began a radical restructuring into one of tenanted farms. By 1852, 14 new holdings had been created and the enclosure of moorland continued, with new fences extending along the slopes of the combes.

One of the striking themes in the reclamation of Exmoor is the strong link between Scotland and Exmoor, consciously made first by John Knight and expanded by Frederic. One of the clearest illustrations of this is in the archaeology of sheep farming on Exmoor.

From July 1868 until the sale of the Exmoor Estate to Viscount Ebrington in 1898, the head shepherd was Robert Tait Little, a Scottish shepherd from the Borders county of Dumfriesshire. He was one of many shepherds from north of the border persuaded by Frederic Knight to bring both family and flocks of Cheviot and Blackface sheep to resettle on Exmoor, as part of his experiment in large-scale sheep ranching. This was to be the last phase of the reclamation of Exmoor. It was made possible by the cultivation of rape as a means of both moorland reclamation and as a feed crop to replace turnips. This method was instigated by Frederick Loveband Smyth who replaced Robert Smith as agent in 1866.

The experiment began at Duredon farm when it came in hand in 1868. Instead of being

Case study
The Pinkery mystery –
the Pinkery Pond and Canal

An abiding mystery in the Exmoor landscape is the feature known as the Pinkworthy or Pinkery Canal. Although described as a 'canal' it is certainly not on that scale, and seems unlikely to have been built to convey boats, though some have suggested this (*see* below). It is best envisaged as a large contour drain and detailed field survey has shown that the canal is some 3m wide and often over 1.5m deep and is embanked on both the upper and lower sides. It follows existing hedgelines along most of its length and runs from Pinkery at the western end of the royal forest along the south-facing slopes between the Exe and the Barle as far as Warren Farm. Although the form of this substantial gulley is damaged in places, particularly towards the eastern end, the canal remains visible as a substantial landscape feature. Aerial photographs from the 1940s and 1950s reveal the canal's original extent demonstrating that most damage is quite recent, probably caused by ploughing in the 1960s and 1970s. From close to the reservoir known as Pinkworthy or Pinkery Pond the canal closely follows the 435m contour south and east for a distance of 9km, ending abruptly above the River Exe at Three Combes Hill.

It is unclear when the pond and canal were made, but it has been suggested that they were cut in the 1820s by Irish labourers imported by John Knight specifically for the task (Burton 1989, 62). What they were made for is even less certain and remains the subject of some debate. It is not known when the name 'canal' was first applied to the channel or even if the individual stretches of ditch were envisaged as a single feature, so no conclusions as to function can be made from the name.

MacDermot (1973, 437) does not mention the canal at all, but discounts the idea that the pond was constructed as a source of power for iron mines yet to be sunk. Instead he felt that the pond was a water supply for farming, a sentiment previously expressed by Orwin and Sellick (1970, 55), who went on to suggest that the canal could only be a failed project to irrigate the area from Pinkery to Honeymead. While acknowledging the impressive scale of the canal, Riley and Wilson-North (2001, 139) consider it to be 'merely a large drainage channel'. Very recent research suggests that the Pinkery Pond and Canal were built to supply the earliest farms at Cornham and Honeymead as well as the designed landscape at Ashcombe (Dr G Wills, pers comm).

A more complex interpretation is based largely on two letters of 1826 and 1829 from John Knight to the agent of Colonel Blathwayt. The pond, canal and proposed Simonsbath to Porlock Railway were visualised as part of a single integrated scheme (Burton 1989; Youell, 1974). The canal was to carry water from the pond to power an inclined plane on the slopes of Three Combes Hill, which would carry the railway over the River Exe. A similar canal-like feature on the northern side of the River Exe, visible on aerial photographs running from Blackpitts to The Warren, would have powered a matching incline roughly

Fig 1.21
Field Survey of Pinkery
Pond and the Pinkery Canal.
[© John Hodgson]

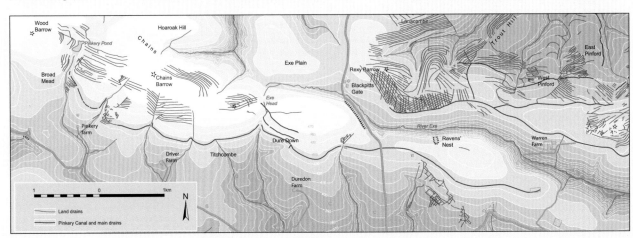

where Warren Farm now stands. A second channel, diverging from this, was possibly intended to fill reservoirs and leats on Porlock Common to power inclines at the Porlock end of the railway (Burton 1989, 65).

A final interpretation flies in the face of all precedent by making the radical proposal that the canal was intended to be exactly that, a canal (Barrett 2004, 36–8). John Knight could have been influenced by innovative late 18th-century industrial transport schemes using narrow canals, such as the Bude canal, or the Stover and Tavistock canals on Dartmoor. Not far from Exmoor the Torrington, or 'Lord Rolle's' Canal, which ran between Bideford and Great Torrington, incorporated a stone aqueduct and incline plane, and was built in the first quarter of the 19th century to connect Torrington with the navigable part of the River Torridge (Hoskins 1954). Such small canals used tub-boats, horse drawn iron or wooden tanks less than two metres wide and sometimes wheeled, capable of carrying 5 or 6 tonnes of cargo. The Pinkery Canal could have accommodated such boats and a watercourse of this size would have

Fig 1.22 (above)
The Pinkery Canal today.
[Rob Wilson-North]

been more than capable of transporting the lime John Knight needed for his moorland reclamations (Barrett 2004, 36). If this idea is accepted, the 'canal' could have linked with the postulated railway inclines which crossed the Exe Valley at Three Combes Hill. In this way, lime could have been conveyed from the railway westwards by boat across the Knight estate as far as Pinkery.

Despite the various interpretations, the Pinkery Pond and Canal remain enigmatic features. However, mapping from air photographs has revealed valuable new

Fig 1.23
'Gutter drains' at
Exe Head.
[RAF/CPE/UK/1980
(RP) Frame 3154
11-APR-1947 Lib 585]

information about their landscape setting. It is clear that the canal was abandoned by the time the new farms at Pinkery, Driver and Duredon were constructed in the 1840s. The line of the canal is cut by many enclosure banks and in places the canal earthworks are reused as hedge-banks for the newly enclosed holdings. However, the field evidence reveals that where the canal is crossed by a new enclosure fence, they are culverted or contain openings, indicating the canal still held water and was kept, at least in part, unblocked (Barrett 2004, 18).

According to Barrett (2004, 27) as the canal was embanked on both the upslope as well as downslope side, it 'would not appear to have been designed to collect surface water running off the slopes from the Chains'. Furthermore, field survey revealed no evidence linking the canal to the

Fig 1.24
The east end of the Pinkery Canal at Three Combes Hill. [RAF/CPE/UK/1980 (RS) Frame 4156 11-APR-1947 Lib 585]

Fig 1.25
The west end of the Pinkery Canal near Pinkery Pond. [OS/73109 (V) Frame 927 29-APR-1973 Lib 10456]

surrounding surface drains, which were in any event associated with Frederic Knight's later farms, and the link between canal and pond made it likely that 'drainage was not the purpose of the project'.

However, it may be inappropriate to think of the canal in terms of a single function. That some later enclosure fences deliberately spanned the canal may indicate that, even if abandoned before being completed, elements of the canal continued to have a function under Frederic Knight, even if not the one originally envisaged by his father. Aerial survey has in fact highlighted several points where connections might have been made between the canal and later reclamations. Frederic Knight's tenants could have integrated the remains of the canal into later farm-scale improvement on an ad hoc basis, appropriating sections either to facilitate drainage, as at Pinkery Farm (SS 7227 4176, SS 7273 4128), or possibly for both drainage and irrigation as at Exe Head. Here, higher contour channels cut parallel to the canal are reminiscent of a large field-gutter water meadow.

Regardless of whether or not the canal could ever have performed any of its suggested functions, or whether those functions will ever be understood, its remains are a significant part of the landscape of improvement on Exmoor.

Fig 1.26
The Pinkery Canal where it deviates from extant field boundaries.
[RAF/CPE/UK/1980 (RS) Frame 4154 11-APR-1947 Lib 585]

tenanted the farm was turned into a herding, with Robert Tait Little installed as shepherd. As more properties became available, they too were added to the number of herdings in the experiment. By 1876 Duredon, Hoar Oak, Winstitchen, Larkbarrow, Cornham, Pinkery and Wintershead each had their own herd and shepherd.

Robert Tait Little was instrumental in introducing the use of sheepfolds, or stells as they were known in Scotland, to Exmoor. Several of these survive, and represent the only upstanding monuments to this important phase of Exmoor's reclamation. The stells can be confidently dated to this period from an entry in the notebook which R T Little kept in his role as head shepherd. In his notebook for the period 1876–1884 he quotes from an earlier influential farming manual, *A Treatise on Practical Store Farming as applicable to the mountainous region of Etterick Forest, and the pastoral district of Scotland in general*, published in 1822 by the Honourable William John Napier, 9th Baron Napier of Merchistoun. Little notes, 'Captain Napier on Store farmering says that sheep without food and shelter is farming on mere chance, that is to say without stells and hay' (Burton 1989, 119–20).

Stells were clearly integral to the Scottish style of 'store farming', which involved the fattening up of lambs and ewes to be sold in the autumn (Sidney 1878, 87). Unlike the earlier pony pounds on Exmoor at Simonsbath, Withypool and Brendon Common outside the royal forest, stells were not simply enclosures in which to gather the beasts for counting. Stells were essential to hill farming in that they were places for the shepherds to provide the sheep with feed and shelter in the harshest of winter weather. By the late 1870s they were established as part of scientific hill farming on Exmoor, operating as part of an integrated system alongside modern mowing and haymaking machinery, which harvested improved hay crops from the new catch meadows, to provided the Cheviot and Blackface flocks with winter feed. In his 'Exmoor reclamation' of 1878 Samuel Sidney reported:

> With the aid of this [mowing and hay-making] machinery, a large quantity of the wild natural forest grass is turned into hay, not of a very fine or nutritious quality, but good enough to keep the ewes or any rough stock alive in hard winters, for mountain sheep will eat and thrive where more luxurious breeds would starve. This hay is stacked and carried to what the Scotch shepherds call 'Stells', for the use of the flocks in hard winters.
>
> (Sidney 1878, 90)

The importance of stells to hill-farming was such that they were included and illustrated in many farming and sheep-management manuals, including the Victorian farmers 'bible', Henry Stephen's *The Book of the Farm*, first published in 1844. Stells could take many forms, and contemporary authors frequently disagreed as to the most effective style. Many of the stells on Exmoor are based on the simplest form recommended by Napier, the circular stell, as described by Little in his notebook:

> A circular stell of dry stone ditch (wall) ten–twelve yards in diameter, with a three ft. open door and six ft. high including cope is the least expensive and most sure improvement that can possibly be adopted.
>
> (Burton 1989, 120)

Captain Napier recommended the creation of a system of stells, placing one in the 'particular haunt' of every part of a flock. To provide protection for all the sheep in a holding, he recommended one stell for approximately every 40 sheep, or 24 stells for every 1,000 sheep. By Frederic Knight's death in 1897 there were over ten thousand sheep in nine herdings on Exmoor (Burton 1989) but the less severe weather than Scotland meant that far fewer stells were needed. Alternatively, it must be remembered that Frederic Knight's foray into sheep-ranching was an experiment, and it might be that this experiment was never completed.

The experimental nature of this enterprise may explain the presence of stells of other design and dimension on Exmoor. For instance, two square enclosures both measuring roughly 45m to a side have been recorded on the east facing slopes of Great Woolcombe. Situated approximately 270m apart, these enclosures may illustrate a trial-by-error nature in stell construction on Exmoor. The easternmost and better preserved of the two might be a direct replacement for the westernmost, which at an elevation 20m higher at about 420m may have proved simply too exposed or too boggy to be useful.

Sheep-drains surround both stells, abutting the earthworks of the higher and probably older stell, but leaving space around the lower enclosure. This might indicate that drains continued to be cut after the first stell had passed out of use, perhaps in an attempt to remedy the boggy state of the higher ground. If stells were indeed introduced to Exmoor by R T Little after 1876, this might indicate that sheep-drains

Fig 1.27
A Scotch Blackface ram.
[Courtesy of C MacGregor]

Case study
Exmoor's sheep stells I

Near Hoaroak Cottage is a circular stell 20m in diameter, which is a close match to the stells proposed by Captain Napier and illustrated in *The Book of the Farm* (described below). Although the earthworks are now bare, the wall of the enclosure was originally topped with hawthorn (Burton 1989, 120). This and the similar stell at Kittuck Meads may have been the earliest stells built by a Scottish shepherd on Exmoor, some time after 1876. The Kittuck stell occupies a ledge at the end of a spur between two combes and its wall is still topped with the grown out beech hedge, planted in the 1870s.

Below Tom's Hill in Long Combe is an oval stell measuring over 35m across at its widest point. It is almost twice the size of the others. Its size may partly be explained by the fact that it encircles a low knoll on the valley floor, which provides additional shelter for sheep. A single entrance lies on the west with a single thorn tree atop the bank to one side.

Two possible stells visible on Great Woolcombe are unusual in both shape and location. These large square enclosures, over 40m across, were built on the exposed eastern slopes of Great Woolcombe. The remains of the lower enclosure survive as earthworks, still topped with a grown out beech hedge. A possibly earlier and abandoned stell can be seen only on aerial photographs, approximately 250m to the west and upslope of the surviving stell.

The Long Chains Combe stell is unusual in that it is irregular in shape and is defined by a faced stone wall and is on a high, rocky knoll above the confluence of Hoaroak Water and a stream rising in the Chains Valley. Such a position would have made it very difficult to drive sheep to, and it has also been suggested as the site of a telling house. It is also possible that this small pound may in fact not be a stell in the Scottish style at all, but one of the earliest sheepfolds on Exmoor, built possibly by John Knight soon after he bought the former royal forest in 1819 (MacDermot 1973, 436). It is the only possible stell on Exmoor other than Buscombe Beeches to show any evidence for a building, the ruined remains of a small hut built into the north-eastern side of the enclosure.

Recent work in the Hoaroak Valley suggests a new reason for this: that the ruined structure is in fact the remains of an out-building associated with the lost Hoar Oak Cottage, built by John Knight in the 1820s and 1830s to house labourers in the forest. Riley (2013) suggests that the survival of the enclosure wall, originally a yard in front of the cottage, might be due to its use as a stell only after the cottage passed out of use.

Fig 1.28
The stell at Hoaroak meads.
[NMR 26882/005]

Fig 1.29 (right)
The stell at Kittuck Meads
with standing beech trees,
March 2011.
[Photo courtesy of Exmoor
National Park Authority]

Fig 1.30 (below)
The stell between Pinford
and Tom's Hill.
[© Rob Wilson-North]

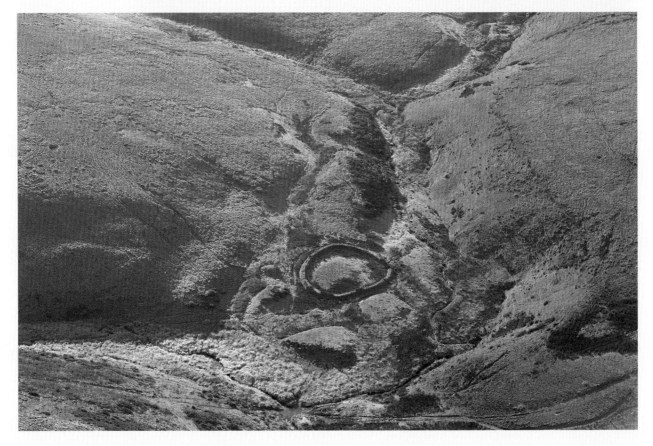

Fig 1.31 (left)
The square stells at Great
Woolcombe. The older
(unfinished) stell is
respected by later drains.
[RAF/106G/UK/1655 (RP)
Frame 3413 11-JUL-1946
Lib 426]

Fig 1.32 (below)
The stell at Long Chains
Combe.
[NMR 1459/376 SS7442/1
01-MAR-1979]

continued to be cut well into the last years of the reclamation of Exmoor.

The evolution of the stell on Exmoor may have reached both its practical and aesthetic peak with the large rectilinear enclosure on the south-facing slopes of Lanacombe, also known as Buscombe Beeches. At its widest points it measures approximately 100m long and 75m wide, enclosing an area of about three-quarters of a hectare, with an entrance on the west side. It has concave sides and at each corner stubs of bank project by 8m, on which are grown-out beech hedging. It is entirely different and argu-ably more elegant in character than all of the other stells. It is this character which has in the recent past inspired an interpretation that, while grudgingly acknowledging a practical purpose, has perhaps over emphasised the aesthetic com-ponent of the enclosure's construction. Roger Burton states:

> This truly artistic piece of work suggests (at least it does to me) the influence of Frederic Knight's lovely wife, whose un-doubted tal-ents were a great blessing to her husband.
> (1989, 120)

As part of John Knight's estate aspirations, the Buscombe Beeches stell undoubtedly enhanced the landscape. However, the influ-ence of authors such as John Napier, Henry Stephens and John Fairbairn, author of *A Trea-tise upon breeding, rearing and feeding Cheviot and Black-faced Sheep in High Districts* under the pseudonym A Lammermuir Farmer, pub-lished in 1823, are more discernible than that of Mrs Knight. For instance, in *The Book of the Farm* Stephens states:

> Instead of the small circular stell, Mr Fair-bairn recommends a form without plant-ation, having 4 concave sides, and a wall running out from each projecting angle.
> (Stephens 1854, 462)

This was a type known as an 'outside' stell, whereby sheep did not enter the enclosure but instead sheltered on the outside of the struc-ture. The concave sides were intended to deflect away the wind and the protruding arms to pro-vide 'succour' against bad weather regardless of wind direction. Being a Dumfriesshire man, R T Little may already have been familiar with the type of stell promoted by Fairbairn. Indeed, sev-eral examples strikingly similar to Buscombe Beeches have been recorded in the Borders area, in the neighbouring former county of Roxburghshire, indicating a direct link between Exmoor and the Borders region.

Owing to the lack of tree planting along the walls, Stephens and others levelled criticism at the shelter provided by this form of stell. Experience had taught hill-farmers that tree plantations provided valuable shelter, 'what the hill countryman expressively calls "succour"' (Acland and Sturge 1851, 29) for both farmer and the farmed, and well-placed beech hedges were considered valuable plantations in their own right. It was around this time that Frederic Knight also established such shelter belts around farmsteads such as Larkbarrow. Without such protection snow could be dumped within stell walls in a blizzard. If used as an 'outside' stell this mattered little, but if the interior was also to be used as shelter, what Stephens calls a 'double' stell, this could pose a danger to sheep sheltering within. That the elaborate Buscombe Beeches stell was planted with beech trees, if only partially, may simply be an aesthetic affec-tation, reflecting the 'comfort and respectability' that planting was also seen to bring to any rec-lamation project (Acland and Sturge 1851, 29). It is more likely, however, that the planting served both a practical and aesthetic purpose, giving additional protection around the corner projections. As Stephens (1854, 461) says in *The Book of the Farm*, in relation to another type of double stell, 'Stells of this construction, besides affording shelter, would form embellishments to a pastoral country'.

Although similar in form to those advocated by Fairbairn, the Lanacombe stell is four times larger in area and was probably an innovation intended to provide 'succour' for several hun-dred sheep, both inside and out, possibly again demonstrating the experimental nature of Frederic Knight's sheep-ranching, and his com-mitment to developing the technology behind improvement on Exmoor.

By the end of the 1870s the 'Scotch' style of sheep-ranching on Exmoor had proved to be viable. In addition, improved rail transport from the station at South Molton allowed Exmoor mutton to be transported to new markets, even as far as London (Orwin and Sellick 1970). More permanently improved pasture was required to meet this increasing demand, and this was an opportunity for Fred-eric Knight to apply cutting-edge technology to the reclamation.

Case study
Exmoor's sheep stells II

'At the commencement of the fall' says Mr Napier, 'the sheep accustomed to the stells would naturally draw forward and reach them with little exertion, and there they would remain in safety, satisfied with the hay with which the stell is stored. When the sleet and snow drive fiercely down the glens, they seek for shelter in the *stell*; but the blast gone by they return to their labour among the snow'.

(Youatt 1837, 292)

But in a storm, their provender cannot be given to sheep upon snow, safely and conveniently, as ground-drift may blow and cover both: and no place is so suitable for the purpose as a stell, a term according to Dr Jamieson, literally signifying a covert or shelter.

(Stephens 1854, 461)

a

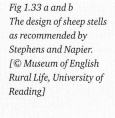
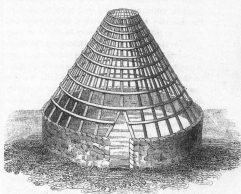

Fig 1.33 a and b
The design of sheep stells as recommended by Stephens and Napier.
[© Museum of English Rural Life, University of Reading]

b

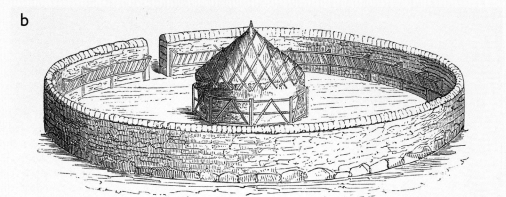

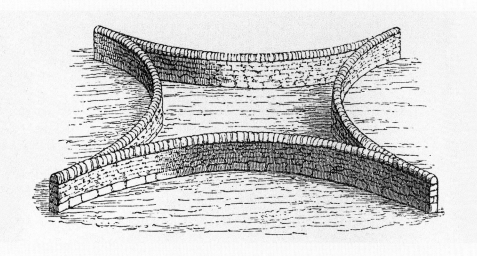

Fig 1.34
Stephens' design of a bastioned sheep stell from his Book of the Farm.
[© Museum of English Rural Life, University of Reading]

Fig 1.35
The stell at Lanacombe known as Buscombe Beeches, with grown out beech hedging on the corner projections.
[NMR 15606/26 SS7842/2 14-JAN-1997]

Fig 1.36 (below)
A number of stells are visible in this aerial photograph of the summit of Bleak Law in the Borders region of Scotland. This is the area from which Frederic Knight drew many of Exmoor's shepherds, including his head shepherd, Robert Tait Little, who was responsible for introducing stells to Exmoor. The two small circular stells are the simplest form, but the large square stell is strikingly similar to that found at Lanacombe.
[RCAHMS SC 569160.
© Crown Copyright: RCAHMS. Licensor www.rcahms.gov.uk]

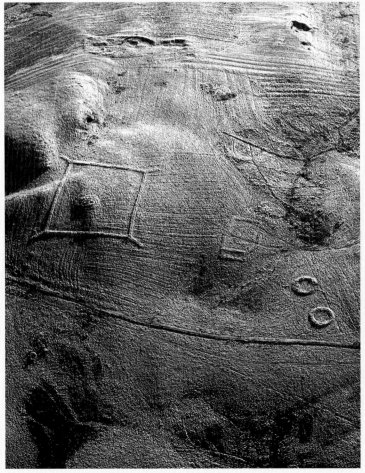

Sheep stells were introduced to Exmoor by shepherds from the Borders region of Scotland, perhaps familiar with winter weather far worse than that usually experienced on Exmoor. However, Exmoor was not immune from bad winters. Abnormally severe snowstorms in March 1878 resulted in the death of nearly 600 sheep from across the estate, roughly an entire steadings worth of animals lost in one night for want of food and shelter (Burton 1989, 119). It was after this experience that stells were built and became an essential part of hill farming on Exmoor, allowing shepherds to provide the sheep with feed and succour even in the harshest of conditions.

Stells took many forms, and many of the Exmoor stells are based on the simplest type, the circular or 'open' stell, recommended by Captain Napier and in Henry Stephen's *The Book of the Farm*. In these, hay could be provided as a stack in the centre or in troughs around the perimeter, ensuring that every sheep had access to a food supply.

A Borders farmer writing under the pseudonym A Lammermuir Farmer, John Fairbairn recommended building stells in 'a form without plantation, having 4 concave sides, and a wall running out from each projecting angle'. This accurately describes the form of Buscombe Beeches enclosure at Lanacombe.

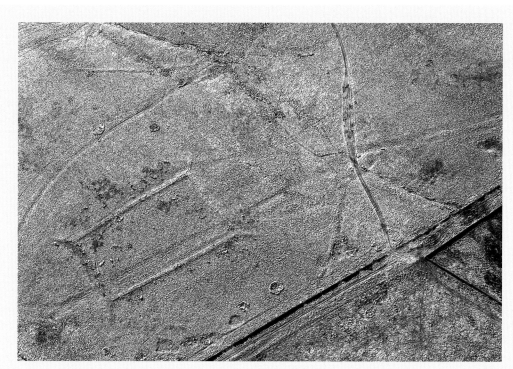

Fig 1.37
A second example with an even greater resemblance to Buscombe Beeches can be found only a few miles from the first away at Bleak Fell, suggesting a direct link between the two areas.
[RCAHMS SC 1203671.
© Professor D W Harding.
Licensor www.rcahms.gov.uk]

Fig 1.38 (below)
A reconstruction of the Buscombe Beeches stell in use.
[© John Hodgson]

'Adventures of a Steam-Cultivator on its journeys through Devonshire Lanes and over Somersetshire Moors'

In 1873–4 the success of the new system of sheep-farming on Exmoor, with its attendant green crops of rape, had made urgent the necessity of breaking-up and subsoiling extensive tracts of wet peat-land, and converting them into permanent pasture … The time seemed to have arrived for trying if steam could not do quickly, effectively and economically, what ox-teams had done slowly and expensively in 1824.

(Sidney 1878, 91)

The use of a steam plough in the reclamation of Exmoor was first described by Samuel Sidney in 1878, from where the above quotation and heading for this section were taken (Sidney 1878, 91–3). More recently this unusual experiment was recounted by Orwin and Sellick (1970) and Burton (1989). Perhaps because the image of a traction engine on Exmoor is so striking, the contrast between the mechanical and the natural so vivid, this episode in the reclamation of the former royal forest lives on in local folklore and has achieved almost mythical status in local history. However, detailed and accurate information about this venture is scarce. It seems that in the absence of such information, the significance of this process in the broader experiment may have been overemphasised. Current archaeological research is enabling these ideas to be given a more balanced perspective.

What is true, although less well appreciated is that the use of steam power in the reclamation of Exmoor provides another link, technological and ideological, between Scotland and the Exmoor reclamations. In particular, the Exmoor reclamation was directly influenced by the most ambitious and expensive reclamation project ever to take place in the British Isles, the Sutherland reclamations in the Scottish Highlands. Whether this was a wise course to take remains open to debate.

A head of steam

A desire for an alternative to animal draught power had been growing among farmers since the early 19th century when, as a result of the Napoleonic Wars, animal feed became very expensive. Concerns over the expense of keeping draught animals persisted into peacetime, but the application of steam power to agriculture became a national obsession in the 1850s and 1860s, encouraged by events such as the Great Exhibition of 1851 and the increasing number of agricultural shows at which manu-

Fig 1.39
The waterwheel at North Furzehill. Such waterwheels powered an array of farmyard machinery.
[© Richard Robinson]

facturers demonstrated their steam-powered wares (Brown 2009).

Nonetheless, with very few exceptions steam technology was rarely taken up unless it was economical and practical to do so. Water power was considered a cheap alternative to animal power for many farmyard tasks, and was in widespread use on Exmoor by the 1850s. For instance, in establishing himself at Emmett's Grange, Robert Smith stated: 'as I have every facility for water power, I propose cutting up the majority of my corn crops for cattle, thereby saving the carriage of the corn to market, raise a good supply of farmyard manure, and let the general produce of the farm be transformed into meat and walk to market' (Acland and Sturge 1851, 31).

With an abundant water supply and the difficulties of transporting fuel around Exmoor, there was little motivation to adapt steam power to common farmyard tasks. In addition, the main impetus for progressive farmers to develop steam power was to reduce overheads in arable cultivation, and it was in this direction that the development of the technology was directed, often with the patronage of aristocratic estates (Brown 2009, 61).

Steam reclamation

It was soon recognised that this new power source could be applied to reclamation (Brown 2009, 105). The first experiments in Britain to make effective use of it were carried out by the Duke of Sutherland on his Highlands Estate, which covered 90 per cent of the former county of Sutherland. He was probably inspired by a demonstration by an employee of the manufacturer Fowler & Co. of Leeds, on a cotton plantation on the banks of the Nile, demonstrating the increasingly commercial and international nature of agriculture in this period. However, the motivations behind the Sutherland reclamations were more complex. Much of the Sutherland estate had been turned over to sheep-walks following some of the most brutal highland clearances of the 1820s, themselves profit-led estate improvements thinly disguised as social experiments. Nonetheless, by the 1860s it was becoming apparent that the clearances had failed to produce the expected long-term revenue increases, largely due to a want of good-quality feed. The Duke of Sutherland's primary motivation in employing steam power in reclamation was therefore probably

financial, as increasing the amount of arable acreage available would permit sheep farmers to winter their livestock on his estate rather than taking them elsewhere, so boosting his rental returns (Tindley 2009, 4).

It is likely, however, that other factors influenced his decision. The duke was an exception to the rule of the pragmatic and practical farmer, employing new technology only where necessary; he was a 'man besotted by steam trains, fire engines and gadgets' (Richards quoted in Winter 1999, 73). In combination with almost endless funds he was keen to apply the new technology to his estate, and apply it he did, with some enthusiasm. From his first trials in 1871 to 1886, a total of 1,405 hectares were reclaimed by steam power, at a cost of £210,870 (Tindley 2009, 10). The vigour with which the Sutherland reclamations were pursued resulted in them becoming internationally renowned, covered by both local and national press and described in detail by the journal of the Royal Agricultural Society. The duke is even thought to have had a hand in designing a new piece of equipment to deal with the unique challenges presented by the peaty and rocky conditions on his estate. The 'Sutherland Reclamation plough' was a subsoil plough combined with stone-hook, constructed and sold by Fowlers. Owing to its fearsome appearance, it soon became known as the 'Duke of Sutherland's Toothpick' (Brown 2009; *see* Case study: Steam-powered reclamation). However, as the cost of the Sutherland reclamations spiralled towards the end of the 1870s and it became clear that the agricultural benefits were actually limited, the publicity continued. Some critics bemoaned the money they saw being squandered, but others simply changed their emphasis, presenting the duke as a patriot rather than a spendthrift:

> there is reason to believe that, in these great enterprises, the Duke of Sutherland has been actuated by public spirit and patriotism, in the highest and purest sense of the word, much more than by commercial considerations.
> (*John O'Groat Journal*, 1874 quoted in Tindley 2009, 308)

It was against this background of both economic and patriotic improvement that Frederic Knight would have viewed the option of steam technology. Given such widespread publicity, even with no evidence of a direct communication between Sutherland and Exmoor, it is

a

unsurprising that the former should inspire the latter. Besides, the firm of Fowlers continued to feature the Sutherland reclamations in their publicity material well into the 20th century, and it is likely that the subject might have arisen at local agricultural shows (Brown 2009). Indeed, it was at one such show, the 1875 Royal Show at Taunton, that Frederic Knight placed an order with the firm of Barford and Perkins for a Fowler's Sutherland Reclamation plough, a four-furrow balance plough and a 10-horse-power traction engine. Exmoor had entered the steam age.

Where the moor is very thick the pan cannot be broken by an ordinary plough, and here a Sutherland plough has been used and enormous furrows of 21 to 24 inches depth have been turned over. A few main drains cut

Fig 1.40a–d
No images of Knight's system in use have been found, but it must have appeared very similar to the Duke of Sutherland's highland reclamations.
(a) Savage of King's Lynn's Agriculturalist traction engine; (b) Fowler's Sutherland Reclamation plough, or the 'Duke of Sutherland's Toothpick';
(c) the 'toothpick' in use;
(d) Fowler's balance plough
[© Museum of English Rural Life, University of Reading]

b

c

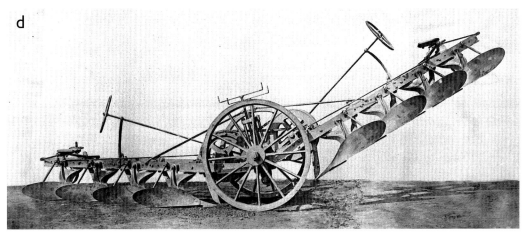

d

across these furrows carry off the water, the peat rots and dries up, and the land is brought into cultivation.

(W C Little, quoted in Orwin and Sellick 1970, 133)

By the time Frederic Knight's sheep-ranching experiment was underway in the 1870s, fierce competition between manufacturers had led to 'indirect traction' emerging as the most wide-spread method of steam cultivation. This used traction engines positioned at the headlands or sides of the field to pull the plough back and forth by rope or cable, thereby avoiding 'panning' or compacting the soil. The Duke of Sutherland's system used two powerful traction engines located on opposite sides of the field, pulling the 'Sutherland Reclamation plough' back and forth to break the peat. However, the Sutherland system was notoriously unreliable and labour intensive, requiring up to 100 men to tend the equipment. Running two large and powerful engines also required substantial quantities of fuel and water, which led a contemporary observer to comment that the Sutherland system 'needed a coalmine in front of them and a river of water behind them in the field where they were at work' (Tindley 2009, 5). A single engine and tackle cost in the region of £1,000 and at the height of his reclamations the Duke of Sutherland had 8 sets of double-engine tackle and 13 general purpose engines (Brown 2009, 105).

For Frederic Knight purchasing two engines would have been expensive enough, and the system also needed parallel roads or tracks to enable the engines to move up and down the field. Frederic Knight's objectives differed from the Duke of Sutherland's in that he wanted to create permanently improved pasture, not arable land, so any tracks he created for a two-engine system would become redundant after the reclamation was complete – an unnecessary expense. Instead he opted for a more econo-mical system which used just one engine, an 'Agriculturalist' traction engine supplied by Savage of King's Lynn, which operated on the 'roundabout' system.

Before 1874 all subsoiling on Exmoor had been 'confined to the dry land by the necessity of being carried out by horse or oxe teams, a slow, laborious and expensive task'. The reclaimed land was converted to permanent pasture to be added to the existing holdings (Orwin and Sellick 1970, 123). Trials of steam-powered subsoiling began in 1876 and were well underway by Christmas of that year, and by the autumn of 1877 'the engine … was in steady work exterminating some 400 acres [162 hectares] of natural forest grass growing on a skin of primeval peat' (Sidney 1878, 93, 95), much of which would previously have been impossible to tackle using conventional means. The method is described in a contempo-rary account:

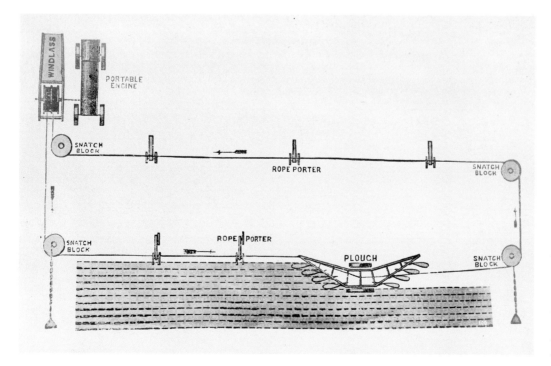

Fig 1.41
A 19th-century schematic diagram illustrating the roundabout system of steam cultivation, requiring only a single traction engine.
[© Museum of English Rural Life, University of Reading]

The Sutherland plough consisted of two huge shares, that is one at each end of the implement, and also at either end a sub-soiler in the form of a fluke of an anchor without palms, the whole resting on four barrel-like wooden rollers which acted as wheels as well as rollers. The engine having been by signal set to work, the plough was slowly dragged forward between two automatic anchors, cutting a huge slice of peat, and making a farrow 12 inches [30cm] deep and nearly 2 feet [60cm] wide; the sod, as it was turned over by the plough, being rolled flat by the barrel wheels. When a double journey had been performed forwards and backwards, the machine was stopped, and one of the hooks let down; and this, in nine cases out of ten, reached, penetrated, and broke up the before-described *pan*, and, with one effort thoroughly dried, and for ever, the peat which had already been destroyed by being torn from its roots.

(Sidney 1878, 93–4)

This process opened up new areas to the ranching experiment. The peat-bogs for which Exmoor was infamous, and which were considered to be one of the worst classes of marginal land, were conversely also seen to be the 'most capable of improvement and after treatment the most valuable land' (William C Little, Assistant Commissioner for Somerset to 1879, Royal Commission on Agriculture, quoted in Orwin and Sellick 1970, 133). Indeed, Sidney states that 'In the opinion of one of the most experienced land-agents in north Devon, the one operation just described doubles the value of the land' (Sidney 1878, 94).

However, precisely where the steam tackle was employed on the former royal forest, and exactly how much ground was broken in this way, remains poorly understood. Orwin and Sellick provide only a general indication, stating that several hundred acres were broken up and reclaimed on Duredon, Titchcombe, Prayway and Ashcombe (Orwin and Sellick 1970, 129). The absence of more detailed

Fig 1.42
An area of straight drains at Squallacombe near Cornham Farm.
[OS/73087 (V) Frame 621 14-APR-1973 Lib 10455]

Case study
Steam-powered reclamation

In 1875 Frederic Knight purchased an 'Agriculturalist' traction engine made by Savage of King's Lynn to operate a Fowler's Sutherland Reclamation plough, known as the 'Duke of Sutherland's Toothpick'. He also bought a general-purpose four-furrow balance-plough. From a stationary position at the field edge the engine drove the plough back and forth by a complex system of cables, pulleys and windlasses. Because this equipment, known as 'the tackle', was arranged around the outside of the field, this type of steam-cultivation became known as the 'roundabout' system, and Fowler's of Leeds became the best known manufacturer of tackle for these systems (Brown 2009, 64).

By the novel means of jacking the engine up and using its rear wheels to drive the cable, the Savage system did away with the need for a separate winding drum, reducing the overall cost. Sidney also claimed that the 'Barford & Perkins' equipment that Frederic Knight purchased could, under the right conditions, be worked for half a day by only two men and 'The engine works with a very small quantity of coal' (Sidney 1878, 93). Nonetheless, transporting even a small amount of coal to unimproved areas of Exmoor must have been a challenge, although a supply of water is never very far away.

The permanently improved farmland pasture of the Exmoor estate is the legacy of this dramatic episode. Only two pieces of circumstantial evidence indicate that this area was, however fleetingly, at the cutting edge of agricultural innovation. The first is

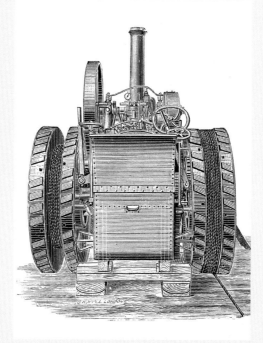

Fig 1.43 (right)
A rear view of the 'Agriculturalist' traction engine, showing the winding gear incorporated into the rear wheels.
[© Museum of English Rural Life, University of Reading]

Fig 1.44 (below)
An 1870s advertising engraving of the 'Agriculturalist' traction engine operating on the roundabout system.
[© Museum of English Rural Life, University of Reading]

hidden in the fabric of two cottages in Simonsbath, which were originally built by Frederic Knight as sheds to house his 'Agriculturalist' engine. The second is in the name of one of the entrances used by the steam engine to reach Titchcombe, although probably very few people recognise this as they pass through the unremarkable 'Engine Gates' today (Burton 1989, 228, 103).

Fig 1.45 Engine Gates near Titchcombe.
[© Rob Wilson-North]

Fig 1.46
West Gate Cottages at Simonsbath.
[© Exmoor National Park Authority]

Fig 1.47
A nameplate from the ploughing tackle purchased by Frederic Knight, recovered from an Exmoor field.
[Courtesy of Alan Vigars]

Case study
The landscape of reclamation at Larkbarrow

In the laying out of a hill farm which shall be chiefly dependent on its own resources, it is found best to divide the land into three classes.

First, the hill-top and other rough land should be set out in one block as summering ground for young cattle, store sheep, colts, ponies &c, to be subsequently improved by 'surface drainage', similar to the Scotch plan of 'sheep-drains' – an inexpensive process yet found of infinite value.

The second or middle class of land to be set out is the portion lying immediately below the wet rough ground or situated upon a southern aspect; these lands are intended for arable culture.

The third land consists of the flats and marshes in the valleys, together with some portions of the adjacent hillsides, which should be laid out for pasture and water-meadows.

(Smith 1856, 355)

The ruins of Larkbarrow Farm lie in a remote combe high on Exmoor and are reached today by a lonely track across moorland. From a distance a scatter of beech trees is all that is left of the shelter belts planted around the farm buildings, and all around are the traces of abandoned field banks and field gutters. This is a relict landscape of reclamation dating from the mid-nineteenth century. In the 1840s Frederic Knight built fences to enclose the wild moorland landscape for the first time, but the act of enclosure was only the first step.

The first tenant to be attracted to Larkbarrow by the low rents was Farmer Hayes from Exford. He took on the farm in 1846 but until 1849 the only structure to be built here was Larkbarrow Cottage. However, the terms of the lease demanded that improvements be made. The sheep-drains on Kittuck Meads and Swap Hill might have been early improvement made by Hayes, draining the pasture as 'summering ground for young cattle, store sheep, colts, ponies' as advocated by Smith.

The farmstead and smaller fields were made by 1850, probably from stone hewn from the ballast quarry next to the paddock fence. The location was carefully chosen. Situated on the south-facing slopes of Kittuck Meads, the farmstead and paddocks were well placed to make the most of the available sunlight and take advantage of the plentiful water supply in Long Combe. The farmstead was enveloped in a plantation of young beech trees which, when mature, would provide much needed 'succour' to the inhabitants, as well as 'an air of comfort

Fig 1.48
The landscape around Larkbarrow Farm. Most of the features of the landscape – the farmstead, fields, tracks, shelter belts, quarries, gutters and peat cuttings – represent the enclosure of the ground and the making of the new farm in the middle of the 19th century.
[© John Hodgson]

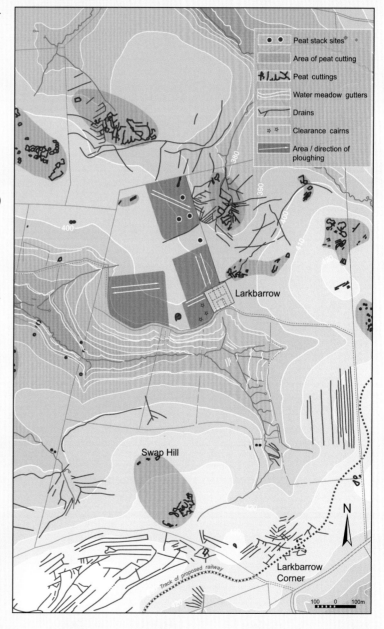

Fig 1.49 (above)
On the track that leads
to Larkbarrow Farm.
[© John Hodgson]

Fig 1.50
Larkbarrow in the 1980s.
[Exmoor National Park
Authority]

and respectability' (Acland and Sturge 1851, 29).

As the first tenant of such a new and modern farmstead, James Meadows would have been keen to make his mark. He made a concerted effort to make this new enterprise a going concern during the two short years in which he was there. Local tradition suggests he grew wheat during his short stay (Orwin and Sellick 1970, 95) and the remains of field clearance cairns and ploughing in the adjacent fields certainly indicate that he wasted no time in breaking new ground.

Meadows seems to have kept Devon cattle on the farm, which were used both for beef and dairying. He also made what Sir Thomas Acland described as an 'excellent Stilton cheese'. Lewis Knight also wrote: 'I have got a cheese, a Stilton, made on the forest, which Frederic thinks will be rich and good.'

Water management was an intrinsic part of the planned farm on Exmoor. Cutting extensive catch meadows in Long Combe seems to have been the last investment made at Larkbarrow before it was taken in hand by the estate in 1851.

Fig 1.51
Larkbarrow Farm.
[26880/028]

records has led to assumptions that the drains of the high moor are the result of steam reclamation. However, the constraints inherent in steam-powered reclamation mean this technique could not have created the often very long and curved drains visible on aerial photographs covering the Chains, Lanacombe, Trout Hill or Woolcombe: steam ploughs were best suited to level ground and could only operate in straight lines. Other than a few small areas of very straight and parallel drains, such as that at Squallacombe, hardly any of the visible drains could have been created by the Sutherland Reclamation plough.

The channels on the high moors are evidence of an earlier, although possibly long-lived, method of drainage. In contrast, steam ploughing proved to be a short-lived and relatively minor aspect of the wider process, which has left little evidence in the landscape. Once subsoiling had been completed, the ground would have been cross-ploughed and harrowed, and then followed by several crops of rape. This would have erased all evidence of 'The Duke's Toothpick' even before the ground was laid to pasture. The legacy of the steam plough on Exmoor is the pasture itself, enclosed below the moorland edge around Duredon, Titchcombe, Prayway and Ashcombe.

Steam ploughing ended on Exmoor around 1880, probably due to the agricultural depression of the 1870s and 1880s. However, some have attributed it to the passing of Frederic Knight's son, whose premature death removed any motivation to improve the estate for posterity. But as Orwin and Sellick state, further areas at Titchcombe were reclaimed after this tragedy. Other large reclamation projects also suffered at this time. For instance, by the end of the 1880s several thousand acres of reclaimed ground on the Sutherland estate were already reverting to rough pasture (Brown 2009). Frederic Knight simply began this great venture too late. In 1876 reclaiming just 8 hectares on the west side of Titchcombe cost over £31, of which nearly £9 went to pay for the eight and half tons of coal required to fire the engine (Sidney 1878, 95). This expense could be justified at the height of farming on Exmoor, but steam reclamation was just too expensive in a depression. By all accounts Exmoor farmers weathered this difficult period better than many, but there was now no incentive to break new ground and the steam tackle was laid up, never to be used again.

Section 2

The commons

The origins of the commons

The origins of common land is a most obscure problem in English History.
          (Hoskins and Dudley Stamp 1963, 5)

What are commons? Put simply, the commons are the 'waste' which lay outside or beyond those areas regularly cultivated in the medieval and post-medieval manor. All common land was defined legally as waste, but as with the royal forest, not all waste was common land. Equally, common land does not equate to 'public' land. It is a widespread misconception that common land is somehow public property or that it belongs to the community as a whole. In fact the commons have been private property since the 10th or 11th century, first under the ownership of manorial lords and more recently private owners or public bodies. It was only with the Countryside and Rights of Way (CRoW) Act 2000 that the public 'right to roam' on areas including registered commons was established, and then only for recreation. Even now only the owners and the commoners have traditional rights of usage (Everitt 2000, 214–15).

Up to 600,000 hectares of commons survive in England and Wales today – about 4% of the total land area – of which about 13 per cent are in the south-west (Clayden 2003). In the 17th century this figure was closer to 3.5 million hectares, or as much as 30 per cent of the country (Hoskins and Dudley Stamp 1963). This figure refers to the proportion of the country as a whole, not just the countryside, because although the commons were essential to many rural trades and communities, they also formed the basis of many urban industries and industrial areas (Bowden *et al* 2009). Nonetheless, surviving commons in England are mostly in the rural areas of the south-west and in highland zones in the north.

How, when and why did the commons develop?

Throughout the country the origin of commons varies from place to place and period to period, each common reflecting its own unique history (Everitt 2000, 214). There is more certainty about when commons developed. Common pasture is mentioned in Domesday Book and archaeological evidence shows that, at least in the Midlands, the open-field system of agriculture of which they were part was in place well before the Norman Conquest, probably by the 8th or 9th century (Hall 1981). In the south-west, common strip-fields on the Midlands model were rare, but examples such as the Braunton Great Field in Devon existed alongside other methods of agriculture, including smaller common-fields and privately owned infields, cultivated in strips around dispersed farmsteads and hamlets. Areas of rough outfield pasture, which was periodically ploughed and cultivated, could be held in common or privately owned, but either way it is clear that systems of 'convertible husbandry' were established in Devon long before the Norman Conquest (Turner 2007).

Domesday Book indicates that common pasture was widespread around Exmoor by 1066. For instance, pasture measuring 4 leagues by 2 leagues [2 by 1km] was recorded at Winsford, probably on Winsford Hill, 3 leagues by 3 leagues [1.6km square] at Molland and 2 leagues by 2 leagues [1km square] at Almsworthy (Siraut 2009, 36–7; *V.C.H. Devon, I.* 409; *V.C.H. Som. I* 437–8, 446, 484, 488–9, 502, 509).

A boundary charter for Ayshford and Boehill, also in Devon, proves that common pasture existed in the south-west by the mid-10th century. In a postscript to the perambulation the charter states that 'Then beyond the common pasture here is the paved road. Then there are many hills that a man may plough' (Turner

Case study
Brendon common – livestock management and enclosures

An enclosure at the head of Lank Combe may be the remains of a pound built to manage livestock on Brendon common. The date of the enclosure is unknown, but it is possible that it was a stock pound used by the Brendon commoners for many years, perhaps since the medieval period. It is well sited in that the combe forms a natural funnel along which livestock could be driven to the pound at its head. It encloses roughly 1 hectare and with the stream which rises within it, 'the main essentials for impounding stock were taken care of' (Burton 1989, 78).

John Knight acquired Brendon common in 1820 and it is probable that the Brendon commoners viewed this purchase with suspicion (MacDermot 1973, 435; Orwin and Sellick 1970, 46). The construction of the nearby wall, between Brendon common and the Badgworthy enclosure, could have been perceived as a prelude to the wider enclosure of the commons and the loss of commons rights. Stories that Brendon commoners pulled the wall down as quickly as it could be rebuilt may be true (Burton 1989, 78). Such actions would not have been illegal as a case from 1500 states 'If I have a right of common and he who hath the land makes a hedge on the land, whence the right of common issues, I may break down the whole hedge' (Clayden 2003, 38). Two ruined structures – one stone built and the other turf built – next to the Knights' enclosure wall may be the remains of shelters built by John Knight for his stockmen to keep an eye on the Brendon commoners (Burton 1989, 78).

The origins and function of the angled wall to the west are unknown. This ruinous boundary appears to have originally abutted the forest wall to the south and is aligned on the Badgworthy wall to the east. Perhaps it repre-

Fig 2.1
This roughly D-shaped enclosure might have sheltered the livestock of the Brendon commoners since the medieval period.
[NMR 26881/027]

sents a later attempt by John Knight to extend his enclosure on Brendon common, or even to build a second pound? A pound on Brendon common is described as suffering a similar fate to the Badgworthy wall (Burton 1989, 78).

Ultimately the fears of the Brendon commoners were needless. From the 1860s the tide of opinion began to turn against the enclosure of commons and Brendon common remained unenclosed.

Fig 2.2 (left)
The Forest wall, visible here at the bottom of Hoccombe Combe would have been a recent intrusion on the previously open landscape when John Knight built the Badgworthy enclosure wall. Both might have been viewed with suspicion by the Brendon commoners, prompting the construction of watchmen's huts to keep watch over the commoners. [RAF/540/931 (RP) Frame 3072 08-NOV-1952 Lib 1324]

Fig 2.3 (below)
The slight remains of buildings near the enclosure wall on Brendon common may be a reminder of tense times as the commoners resisted the unlawful enclosure of the common. [© Rob Wilson-North]

2007, 42; *see* Finberg 1971, 23). It was in areas such as the south-west, where classic common-fields agriculture was just one component in a complex landscape of scattered farmsteads and hamlets, that commons were most extensive, and the moorland of the south-west is 'prominent among those areas' (Everitt 2000, 214).

The development of the commons is linked to the evolution of common rights. For Exmoor this is intrinsically linked to the creation and function of the royal forest. It has been argued that common rights might have first been granted as compensation for the loss of other property rights when a royal forest was created. For example, when William I enlarged the New Forest in 1079, he seems to have granted common rights to those people now governed by forest law. However, it seems unlikely that William I would have been so considerate (Hoskins and Dudley Stamp 1963, 5–6).

Similarly, MacDermot (1973, 2) suggests that the creation of Exmoor's commons was in part driven by the process of the forest becoming Crown land. Common grazing on the moors probably predates the creation of the royal forest. It is likely that the formalisation of the Exmoor commons simply recognised this established tradition 'of turning out their cattle on the great waste at their doors and of taking fuel there' (MacDermot 1973, 2). It is possible that the extent of the Exmoor commons was defined by the area over which the local inhabitants' livestock naturally ranged from their settlements (MacDermot 1973, 2).

Establishing the boundaries of the commons would have been necessary so that the royal forest officials could distinguish the commons from the forest. A clear boundary would define the area for which fees could be levied for the agistment of livestock and fines charged for transgressions against forest law, although as the size of the royal forest changed, this was often a matter of dispute.

The creation of the royal forest, therefore, did not create Exmoor's commons, but it did help to crystallise and reinforce the rights of common that were already in place, rights which were possibly older than the concept of private property itself (Hoskins and Dudley Stamp 1963, 5–6; MacDermot 1973, 203).

Boundary markers of the commons

By the 13th century many of Exmoor's commons were under forest law, but once the neighbouring manors gained control of their commons after disafforestment (in 1204), it was vital that that all commoners knew where the boundaries lay and that they were maintained (Siraut 2009, 74). Some were marked by banks or ditches but many used existing features such as outcrops, trees, standing stones or prehistoric burial mounds, the location of which had to be memorised. The boundaries of the commons were reinforced by inclusion in the regular perambulation of the parish bounds, called 'beating the bounds'. Novel methods were often used to impress the location of the markers on the young. Several are known from early 17th-century court proceedings, but probably reflect much older traditions. The inhabitants of Exford parish seem to have been particularly enthusiastic in making their perambulations memorable. For instance, if one of the boundary stones between Exford common and the royal forest was discovered to have fallen, one elderly resident recalls a boy would be laid on it and given 'gentle blows and pinches'. Another remembers as a boy a neighbour calling him to 'put his finger on a meerestone, saying that that is was soe hot it would scald him' and when he did so the same neighbour 'layd hold of [his] hand and did wring one of his fingers sorely that for the present it grieved him very much, and said "Remember that this is a boundstone and is a boundary to the parish of Exford"' (MacDermot 1973, 353).

Common rights and commons usage

A common right can be broadly defined as 'a right which one or more persons may have to take or use some portion of that which another mans soil naturally produces' (Halsbury's Laws of England, quoted in Clayden 2003, 10). The owner of the common, originally often the lord of the manor, is referred to in legal documents as the 'lord of the soil'. Specific common rights vary greatly from place to place and from period to period, influenced by a range of factors such as the extent of the waste, the type and diversity of resources available and the number of commoners exploiting the common (Everitt 2000, 216).

Just as the commons were not open to everyone, the right to exploit a common's resources was usually restricted to the inhabitants of a particular manor or parish. Often they were even further limited, attached to a particular house or holding within the manor, and could only be used to maintain that 'dominant tenement'. For instance, common pasture was restricted to grazing by livestock from farms in the manor and any peat cut under common of turbary was for domestic use and could not be sold (Winchester 2006). A farm or cottage would have a turf-pit allocated for its own use.

On Exmoor the commoners can be defined as tenants of the manors or parishes bordering the royal forest, the precincts of the suitors at large, and the commoners of the ancient tenements of Withypool and Hawkridge, the precincts of the free suitors (MacDermot 1973, 181; unnumbered figure, 182–3). The duties, or suits, owed by these in return for rights of common on the royal forest are discussed in section 1. It is possible that the rights enjoyed on the forest had been granted to the commoners in return for not harming the king's deer if they were found causing damage on the adjoining commons (MacDermot 1973, 204).

The rights of common

Exmoor's commoners could claim rights of common estover, pannage, piscary, pasture and turbary, mirroring those rights enjoyed by the suitors at large and free suitors on the royal forest. This is not surprising because the commons were unenclosed and the division between the resources of the commons and those of the royal forest a legal, rather than a physical, one.

Evidence from a 13th-century valuation of the royal forest income indicates that pigs were kept on Exmoor forest, and therefore probably roamed on the commons. However, pannage, the common right of feeding animals, usually pigs, on woodland acorns and mast is not listed as an income, perhaps unsurprising given the lack of woodland on Exmoor. It is likely that pannage was not a right widely exercised on the forest or many of the similarly stark commons (MacDermot 1973, 134–5, 222, 302). The rights of piscary and estovers were granted to the free suitors in the forest and the precincts of the 52 ancient tenements, presumably including the manorial commons. Little reference is made to the rights of the suitors at large of piscary and estovers on the wider commons (MacDermot 1973, 184).

The rights of estover, pannage and piscary leave little archaeological trace, but the rights of pasture and turbary leave a lasting landscape legacy. Historically, the right of pasture was arguably the most important common right on Exmoor. The pasture on the commons gave Exmoor's hill farmers the resources to compete with lowland farmers with access to better quality grazing (Siraut 2009, 73). It was probably for this reason that those commoners bordering the royal forest, the suitors at large, could also graze their livestock on neighbouring commons by reason of 'vicinage', whereby the commoners of two adjoining unfenced commons would allow animals to cross each other's boundaries, but not beyond (MacDermot 1973, 203). The right of pasture has left livestock pounds, such as that on Brendon common, as a visible reminder of managing the livestock on the commons. Peat cutting is an invasive and inherently destructive process, and the right of turbary has left an enduring mark on the moorland landscape of Exmoor.

Peat: 'dirty, dirty fire-stuff'

When they were dry, the bottoms, which were jet black, would be just like a lump of coal, and it would last a long time. It was dirty, dirty fire-stuff, but it did the job.
(Victor Lock, quoted in Ramsay 2009, 15)

In comparison to other upland landscapes in Britain and Ireland, peat cutting is a poorly understood and neglected aspect of Exmoor's history. However, aerial photographs reveal just how extensive peat cutting was on Exmoor, both in the forest and on the commons and mapping the extent of old peat workings shows that practically every moorland hilltop from Brendon Common in the north to Withypool Common in the south, and from Ilkerton Ridge in the west to Dunkery Hill in the east was dug over for peat. It has had a profound, and often overlooked, effect on the character of Exmoor's moorland landscape.

Peat cutting on Exmoor is not coordinated or large-scale extraction, as seen in the Somerset Levels or Norfolk Broads (Rotherham 2009). Instead, peat cutting on Exmoor was a cottage industry, almost always done to provide domestic fuel for local consumption. During the 19th century every dwelling on the forest cut a set quota of turves annually from their own dedicated pit; up to 8,000 for a cottage, 20,000 for a farmhouse (Burton 1989, 232–3). One man cutting fuel for his own hearth was expected to cut around 1,000 turves a day. Between one

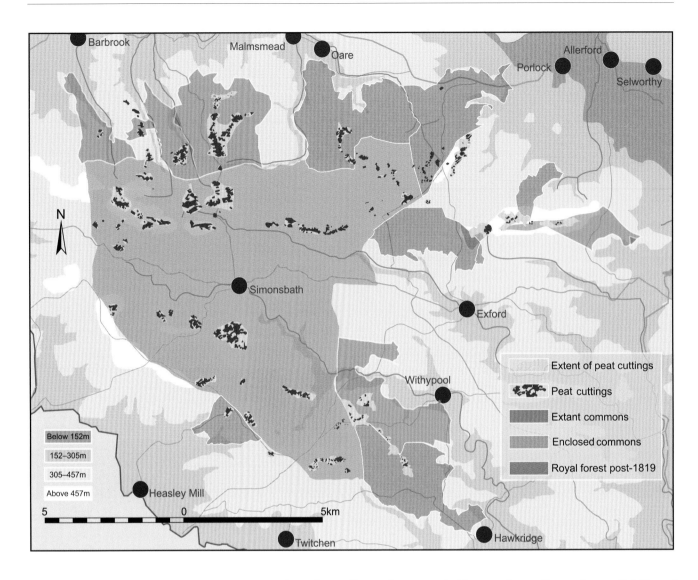

Fig 2.4
Aerial survey has revealed the extent of peat cutting on Exmoor. Small-scale extraction is evident on the royal forest as well as on the surrounding commons.
[© John Hodgson]

and three weeks must have been allocated to this job, fitted in between all other requirements of the agricultural year. However, the time and effort varied with the depth and type of peat being cut.

It is certain that peat cutting has taken place on Exmoor since the medieval period and court records confirm that it remained an important activity on the commons into the 17th century. For instance, in 1678 the deposition of Thomas Lock of North Molton states that 'he has been commonly employed cutting turf in the Forest and on Molland Common' (MacDermot 1973, 359). In fact, it is probable that without the turf for fuel, establishing and maintaining life on Exmoor would have been difficult, if not impossible. Although the common right of pasture may have been economically important, as has been suggested for Bodmin Moor, the viability of many of the moorland edge settlements

probably rested equally on the availability of turf for fuel (Herring et al, 2008).

Peat cutting was an important part of life on Exmoor and, of all the common rights, has left the most enduring mark on many of Exmoor's commons. Each curve or step in the edge of a large pit may be a diagnostic marker, shaped by many generations of the same family over hundreds of years, using the same methods and potentially even the same tools.

The process

The laborious job of cutting turf was sometimes shared between friends and family members, even women and children helping with all but the cutting and hauling. More often than not, however, it was a solitary task carried out 'in-between whiles', when other jobs allowed. Nonetheless, making time for this in the spring

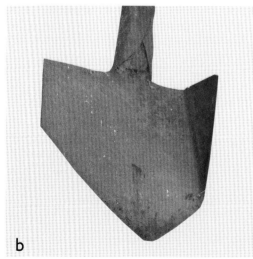

a c

b

after year. The pits of neighbouring farms also tended to cluster, the Brendon farms cuttings for instance, congregating in the area around Brendon Two Gates (Ramsay, pers comm).

The process of turf cutting began with preparing the pit. Using an old or adapted hay or silage knife, a tool normally used for cutting hay out of a stack for animal feed, the vertical face of the existing pit was trimmed and vegetation removed from the surface, to a spade's width, plus standing room. Once the year's cutting was over, these top cuttings were placed in the bottom of the pit to regrow. To ensure consistency in the turf size, a cutting line was often marked about a spade's width or 20–25cm from the cleared edge of the pit. The regularity of the first cut in a new turf pit therefore had the potential to determine the shape of the later pit.

Different tools were used to cut different types of turf. The varying techniques employed may also have influenced the shape of a pit, contributing to the variety in the appearance of the turbaries when seen on aerial photographs.

Exmoor peat is divided into two types and has been given a number of names. First, there is the deep, black peat which is often called pit or peat turf, after the deep pits in which it is cut. Second, the shallow beds that are skimmed from the surface, are described as spine turf, 'skimmies' or more commonly skin turf (Burton 1989, 233; Ramsay 2009, 15; 2010, pers comm; Herring *et al* 2008, 117). Some preferred to cut only the pit turf, which dried hard like coal and burnt slowly, as the thinner skin turf burnt hot, but too fast (Ramsay, pers comm).

Throughout the south-west a tool sometimes called a Devon spade or a Cornish long-handled shovel was used to cut the deeper pit turf, although a turf-iron, similar to those used in the peat bogs of Scotland and Ireland may have been used, as they were on Bodmin (Herring *et al* 2008). For skimming off the shallower skin turf a long handled spade known as a paring iron was widely used, similar to the turfing spades still in use today to cut grass turf (Rotherham 2009). On Exmoor the tools were known simply as the 'pit turf spade' and 'skin turf spade', and examples of these tools can still be seen locally (Figs 2.5 and 2.6). They were probably made in the area, to individual requirements, so no two tools would be exactly the same. However, in general, Exmoor pit turf spades had a straight shaft about 1.5m long with a short handle, and the blade was often slightly curved along its length. Skin turf spades

Fig 2.5 a–c
Examples of Exmoor pit turf spades survive in the Lyn and Exmoor Museum. (c) is Santa Lafuenti's locally made pit turf spade. [(a) and (b) courtesy of Lyn and Exmoor museum; (c) courtesy of David Ramsay and Santa Lafuenti]

was vital. Cutting in April or May would allow the cut turves to dry in the open air of the early summer months.

Convention and personal preference dictated where each farmer or labourer cut their turf. Farmers were free to cut anywhere within reason, but most returned to the same pit year

Fig 2.6
An Exmoor skin turf spade.
[Image courtesy of Lyn and Exmoor Museum. Photographs © David Ramsay/Brian Cox]

Fig 2.7 (far right)
Unlike pit turf spades, skin turf spades were pushed by the turf cutter, like the breast plough or paring spade used in the process of paring and burning. [Image from Henry Stephens' The Book of the Farm, *© Museum of English Rural Life, University of Reading]*

were similar, but often with a more rounded end to the bottom of the blade and a longer, curved 'T' handle at the top, against which turf cutters could push with their stomach, like a breast plough or paring spade.

Tools and techniques may have changed over time and probably even varied from cutter to cutter and pit to pit. Locals recalling the process in the early 20th century describe how the shallow peat deposits were cut diagonally, and the deeper beds cut vertically (Burton 1989; Ramsay 2009). It may be that these different techniques contributed to the varying shapes of the pits. Some are very regular in shape, square or rectangular, suggesting that the first cutting was carefully laid out and the peat cut from straight edges. Others are circular, oval or irregular, abstract combinations of interconnecting pits making it difficult to tell where one pit ends and another begins. Individual trenches can

a

be seen within many of the pits, following the curved edges of the bank, the remains of the most recent extraction, but this makes it all the clearer that many pits have been worked, and perhaps reworked, over long periods.

The size of the turves and the depth of the pit were determined by the length of the shovel and thickness of the peat, which varied from place to place. The thickest peats on Exmoor, reputed to be on Warren Allotment, were over 2m deep, which would have been removed in several spits (Burton 1989, 233). On average, individual turves would have been about 24cm wide and up to 5cm thick, weighing just over 3kg (Ramsay 2009).

Cutting the shallow, fibrous skin turf was laborious work and took more time than the deeper pit turf, but the deep peat was heavy when wet and when drying could be crumbly and difficult to move in one piece. The turves were cut and landed in one fluid motion, and then either left on the bank to dry, or if it was wet, moved by wheelbarrow or dray, a type of horse-drawn sledge, to a higher site where they were laid out to dry. Over the next month or two the turves were regularly checked and turned. When dry, curled at the edges and coal-like in colour, the fuel was ready for 'saving'.

If time allowed, the dry turves were straight-away transported to the farm or cottage by

Fig 2.8
(a, facing page) 'A lonely peat cutter' on Brendon Common in the late 19th or early 20th century, and (b, below) Santa Lafuenti cutting turf on Brendon Common in 1991. Little has changed in this process during the intervening years.
[Courtesy of Michael Berry and © Chris Chapman]

b

horse and cart or dray. However, saving a year's worth of fuel took several days and free time was rare in the busy agricultural year. If the weather was bad, transport wasn't available or the saving of the peat clashed with another, more important task such as the harvest, temporary turf stacks called 'ricks', 'stooks' or 'burrows' could be built on the moorland. First-hand accounts of building turf stacks in the mid-20th century recall that the only protection from the weather provided for them was in the sloping of the turves to shed rainwater (Ramsay, pers comm). In contrast, the diary entries of a Withypool farmer from earlier in the century note the gathering of rushes 'for thatching turf rick', a technique also noted on Bodmin Moor (Herring *et al* 2008; *Diaries of Mr Land*, in the possession of Mr Sanders of Launceston and on loan to Exmoor National Park Authority). While the technique of turf cutting may be largely unchanged, other aspects of the process have clearly evolved.

To date, over eighty possible turf stacks have been recorded on Exmoor. Some may be reused prehistoric burial mounds, and it is likely that more turf stacks remain to be discovered. Similar features have been recorded in most turf-cutting regions of Britain, with directly comparable remains found on Bodmin (Herring *et al* 2008). Other areas developed more long-term and expensive responses, such as the purpose-built peat huts of Eskdale (Winchester 1984). It is interesting to note that these Lake District 'peat scales' each belonged to a particular holding and their location corresponded closely to established routes taken in the regular drifts of sheep from farm to moor. Similar associations remain to be discovered on Exmoor, but the idea raises the possibility that some of the packhorse tracks owe their origin as much to the transportation of peat as the movement of sheep (Herring *et al* 2008).

Once the dried turves had been delivered to the farm or cottage, the fuel needed to be kept dry and accessible. The turves were often re-stacked into huge ricks, either in the yard close to the farmhouse kitchen door, or in special 'turf mowhays'. The centre of the rick was often left hollow to ventilate the stack and the outermost turves were again often slanted outwards to protect them from the rain.

Fig 2.9
Turf stacks on Countisbury Common in 1939.
[Courtesy of Edward Nightingale/Lyn and Exmoor Museum, photograph ©
Dr M P Nightingale]

Some Exmoor farmsteads also incorporate buildings that have been identified by the owners as turf stores. These may be purpose-built or else would have reused existing farm buildings. They tend to be attached to the farmhouse or close to the farmhouse kitchen door. Roy Kellaway, a labourer at the Brendon farm of Higher Tippacott from the 1940s, believed that this was the only farm in the area to have a proper 'turf house'. However, John Pile also recalls an outbuilding across the farmyard from the kitchen acting as turf house at the nearby Hallslake Farm, his home for 70 years (Ramsay, pers comm 2010). Other turf stores have been recently recognised at Cloggs (D Bawden, pers comm) and at North Furzehill where a tall, lean-to structure abutting the threshing barn lies opposite the entrance to the yard from the farmhouse door. At Lyshwell Farm a similar tall lean-to on the end of the house is connected with their kitchen by a hatch so that turves could be passed straight into the kitchen.

Commons and manorial courts

Although valuable, it is important to remember that the resources of the commons were finite. Over-exploitation, particularly through overgrazing, was always a danger and the commons have often been a resource under stress. The land was the property of the lord of the manor, but his ability to enclose and exploit it was restricted by the use-rights of his tenants (Everitt 2000, 216; Winchester 2006, 8). A degree of conflict was perhaps inevitable and some type of communal control was necessary.

The waste was also subject to conflict between commoners. The 'tragedy of the commons' is an idea that suggests commoners would always be tempted to put their own interests before those of the manor, for instance, in grazing numbers of livestock that the common could not sustain. The logical conclusion is that 'freedom in a common brings ruin to all' (Hardin 1968, 1244). But access to the commons was nearly always regulated (Winchester 2006, 4) and they were in fact carefully administered by the manorial courts. These were seigniorial courts held to uphold the lord's rights. As such, it has been suggested that the lord of the manor could do as he pleased in administering the commons (Holtom 2008) although, in fact, manorial courts comprised juries drawn from the leading tenants of the manor, and the byelaws issued by them, for-

malising customs in relation to all aspects of the manor, including the commons, were as binding to the lords as to the tenants (Siraut 2009, 55). The role of the manor court was therefore to reach a balance between maintaining the lord's privileges and ensuring the smooth running of the community.

Fair access to the commons was potentially a source of great tension within the community and was therefore governed by a complex system of byelaws (Winchester 2006). That the 'tragedy of the commons' was avoided is due largely to the manorial courts achieving a degree of sustainability in their administration of the commons.

The 16th and 17th centuries were the heyday of manorial court control. However, it was not a period of universal harmony and manorial records contain evidence that tensions were ever-present, with frequent disputes and breaches of commons byelaws. Pasture rights were particularly disputed. For instance, in 1556 an Exford man was accused of overstocking Riscombe Down with 100 sheep, and it was necessary for the courts to remind Almsworthy tenants of the customary stocking rates on the commons (Siraut 2009, 74). Court records from the 17th century indicate that manorial control ensured that the commons remained in use for 'dominant tenement', at least for pasture. For instance, in 1638 the depositions of two defendants in court at Minehead stated 'if the copyholders [tenants] of Monkham take in the cattle of strangers to depasture on the common, the same is presentable at the

Fig 2.10
Cloggs Farm. The turf store adjoins the farmhouse.
[© Rob Wilson-North]

Fig 2.11
From above, the turf cutting
on Brendon Common
acquires an almost abstract
quality, and is very difficult
to record and interpret.
[OS/73087 (V) Frame 676
14-APR-1973 Lib 10455]

Case study
Peat cutting on the commons

The cutting of turf or peat is one of the central strands in the story of the Exmoor commons. It was not on an industrial scale, but was the work of individuals, of numerous generations, cutting fuel to keep their homes warm and their families fed. It has literally helped to shape the landscape. However, until recently, the extent of peat extraction and its impact on the character of the moor has been largely unappreciated.

An aerial perspective reveals just how widespread peat cutting was (*see* Fig 2.4) and even a brief study of aerial photographs shows how diverse the peat cuttings are. On Brendon Common alone, turf-pits have been identified ranging in size from less than 3m square to well over 100m long. Some are very regular, square or rectangular in shape, suggesting they were carefully laid out and the peat cut from straight edges. Many of the most regular pits are also the smallest, and might have been in use only for a short period. Others are less regular, curving pits or interconnecting pits, which makes it difficult to tell where one pit ends and another begins. These are also the largest pits.

Turf cutting continued on Brendon Common well into the 20th century. Dick French of Brendon Barton was one of the last to exercise his right of turbary on Brendon Common, although the turf was actually cut for him by Jack Buckingham and Santi Lafuenti, who both lived at Simonsbath (Burton 1989, 233; Ramsay, pers comm).

The difference between the individual, irregular and piecemeal turf-cutting pits on Brendon Common, cut under common rights of turbary, and the regular and organised extraction visible on Exe Plain west of

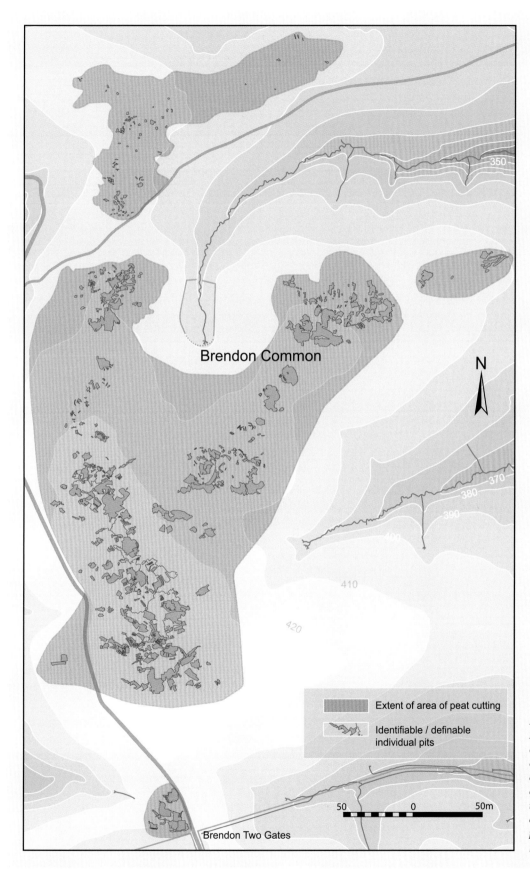

Brendon Common

N

Extent of area of peat cutting

Identifiable / definable
individual pits

Brendon Two Gates

50   0   50m

Fig 2.12
By analysing a range of
aerial photographs taken
at different times of year
and in varying light
conditions, a composite
map can be created that
accurately depicts the turf
pits over a large area.
[© John Hodgson]

Blackpitts, probably associated with the 19th-century expansion of Simonsbath as the centre of the Exmoor estate, is immediately apparent (*see* Case study: Peat cutting in the forest – Blackpitts and the Chains).

An Ordnance Survey aerial photograph of 1973 (*see* Fig 2.11) graphically illustrates both the extent of turf cutting and the challenges in recording turf cuttings from the air. The deeper pits are clearly visible, hard shadows marking one edge and pooling water highlighting individual trenches within them. Some shallower pits, and the full extent of the cuttings, are discernible only through changes in vegetation or surface texture.

Fig 2.13
Turf Cuttings on Brendon Common, c 1950, painted by Viola Gardner who lived at Tippacott.
[© *Viola Gardner; Courtesy of Mike Berry*]

court of the manor and punishable there' (Mac-Dermot 1973, 293).

Unfortunately, documentary descriptions of common rights are rare. A late exception can be seen in an 18th-century survey of Higher Blackland farm near Withypool, which defined the tenant's suits to the forest and his common rights of pasture and turbary. He could cut an unspecified amount of turf for fuel, could keep 14 score (2,800) sheep, 10 mares and foals and could graze as many cattle in summer as could be kept on his holding in winter (SRO, DD/SF 3147).

This survey may provide us with an insight into the evolution of manorial control of common rights on Exmoor. The grazing of upland commons was usually managed in one of two ways. The rule of levancy and couchancy restricted the number of livestock a tenant could pasture on commons in the summer to those he could sustain through the winter on his own holding. It was in theory an unrestricted right, but was in practice limited by the capability of the commoner's holding. The second method was to manage the livestock by 'stint'. Stinting defined the commoner's right to pasture in strictly numerical terms, for instance '14 score sheep' (Winchester 2006, 10).

Levancy and couchancy probably originated in the 'open' wastes, such as forests on which settlement and colonisation were allowed in the 12th and 13th centuries, such as in the Lake District and the north Pennines. This resulted in a landscape of new farms and hamlets in the forest valleys, similar to those around the fringes of Exmoor. In contrast, stinting is associated with 'closed' forests, those over which lordly control was retained and which were often maintained as demesne farms. The primary aim of closed forests was the raising of income through agistment, as with the royal forest of Exmoor. Levancy and couchancy were incompatible with agistment as the number of beasts was limited to those wintered on the farm, thereby limiting the lord's income. In contrast, although stinting placed a limit on the number of livestock, it did not specify where they should come from, and so could be set at a higher rate.

The common rights for Higher Blackland farm appear to contain elements of both these mechanisms, which might reflect the two-tier nature of common rights on Exmoor, with tenants often having rights of common both within the royal forest and on the surrounding manorial commons. Manorial use of levancy and couchancy would maintain a degree of fairness in access to the commons based on the size of the holding. The element of stinting may be a legacy of the origins of the commons as part of the forest, expressing older seigniorial desires to limit the number of tenants' livestock to preserve grazing for 'beasts of the chase' or their own herds (Winchester 2006, 11).

Although partly a type of communal 'folk-meet', the effectiveness of the manor courts' in managing the commons depended on the machinery of manorial administration. As manor courts decreased in importance throughout the 18th century, so did their role in managing the commons. By 1800 most manorial involvement with the commons had ceased (Winchester 2006, 13). This coincided with the changes in how the waste was perceived, which in turn led to progressive landowners, such as the Knights, reclaiming what was previously seen as marginal land. The improvers turned their gaze to the commons, which they viewed as a wasted resource, and as with the royal forest, the precursor to improvement was, inevitably, enclosure.

Enclosure of the commons

Temporary medieval and post-medieval enclosure

Enclosure by act of parliament or parliamentary enclosure is such a well-known and traumatic episode in the English landscape that very often the fact that many commons were lost to enclosure centuries earlier is overlooked. Even some of the commons that appear unenclosed today have gone through episodes of enclosure and cultivation in the past.

Until relatively recently, arable cultivation played a very important role in farming on Exmoor with the amount of land being cultivated varying greatly from farm to farm. Some were almost entirely pastoral but others were required to grow crops to pay rent partly in wheat (Siraut 2009, 91). The commons therefore played a vital role in both the pastoral and arable systems. External considerations such as high grain prices during the Napoleonic Wars or population growth could increase demand and price, pushing agriculture to the fringes of cultivated land. The use of the commons was not confined to the rights of common described above, and at times they too were enclosed and cultivated as temporary outfield.

Case study
Farming the commons –
Molland Moor, Anstey and
Winsford Hill

The commons of Molland Moor, West Anstey and East Anstey lie along an 8km length of the southern escarpment of Exmoor, just beyond the southern extent of the former royal forest. Today only West Anstey remains common land. East Anstey Common was enclosed by act of parliament and partly enclosed in the mid-19th century, and all common rights on Molland Moor reverted to the lord of the manor at around the same time. Nonetheless, the former commons, undivided by fence or wall, covered nearly 12km² (over 1,180 hectares) of open moorland. Across much of this expanse are the traces of abandoned field systems and ridge and furrow ploughing of probable medieval date.

These field systems are very different in character to those small-scale and piecemeal 'rye-banks', which enclose areas of the northern commons. As far as the constraints of local topography allow, these larger and more regular enclosures were planned as blocks of fields, encroaching onto the moors sometimes in a continuation of the enclosure pattern surrounding the waste today. The fields were also laid out to accommodate existing routeways, which suggests a degree of planning and control. It is possible that the field boundaries were built (and perhaps topped with a 'dead hedge') to protect arable crops from animals depasturing on the commons.

However, the commons were not enclosed *en masse*. On the more productive south-facing slopes, two, three or even more phases of enclosure are visible with rows of fields climbing the commons, like steps in a flight of stairs. A clear example can be seen around Tucker's Farm to the north of Molland, where the lowest, and presumably earliest intakes remain enclosed and in use today.

Almost all of the relict fields on Molland Moor, West Anstey and East Anstey commons, even those at the summit, contain ridge and furrow. This ploughing, presumably

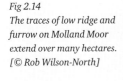

Fig 2.14
The traces of low ridge and furrow on Molland Moor extend over many hectares.
[© Rob Wilson-North]

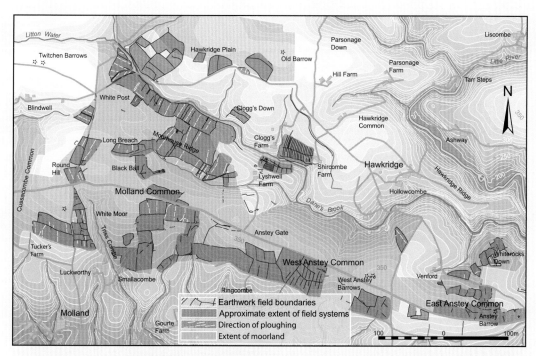

Fig 2.15
From Molland Moor to East Anstey Common, the earthwork remains of abandoned field systems are visible across nearly 12km² of moorland. The mapping of these features from aerial photographs reveals the organised nature of the system.
[© John Hodgson]

Fig 2.16
The commons were cultivated by farms that abutted them, such as Lyshwell, which has existed since the 1300s. Some farms are abandoned and around Lyshwell Farm are the earthworks of four deserted farmsteads.
[NMR SS/8330 28–31 (23426/07) 01-MAR-2004]

Fig 2.17 (below)
The Wambarrows on the top of Winsford Hill – areas of ridge and furrow run up to and override the barrows, extending cultivation to the very summit of Winsford Hill. [NMR 21076/09 SS8734/ 33–34 09-FEB-2001]

Fig 2.18 (facing page) The cultivation of these commons was extensive, and the relict remains of former fields were visible in January 1947 extending into land now enclosed on South Hill. [RAF/CPE/UK/1944 (RP) Frame 3161 23-JAN-1947 Lib 561]

for arable crops, must have been of short duration due to the shallow and unproductive soils. A few seasons and the ground would have been exhausted. Nevertheless, on the scale at which these fields were created the crops would have been a significant contribution to the local economy. A by-product of the ridge and furrow may have been the improved drainage of the ground and perhaps an improved grass crop. The scale of the field systems also implies that the local population was much larger than it has become, and the deserted farmsteads around the commons, such as at North Lyshwell, may go some way to explaining this.

Similar field systems with ridge and furrow are found on the commons of Winsford Hill, South Hill and Varle Hill. Most of this area is above the 350m contour, a situation even more exposed than Molland Moor and Anstey commons. The fields were recorded from the air, but recent field survey (Smart 2002) has confirmed the extent of the ridge and furrow. Interestingly, it also confirmed that most of the ridge and furrow predates the construction of the field boundaries, with many of the enclosure banks actually overlying the ridge and furrow. Local tradition suggests that the ridge and furrow is Napoleonic in date (1799–1815) (Hallam 1978). However, it seems certain that this is evidence of earlier, unenclosed cultivation probably in the medieval period.

The cultivation of the commons was a contentious issue as late as the 17th century. James Boevey's determination to squeeze ever higher profits from the former royal forest reached new levels when, in the 1670s, he claimed the commons as part of the forest. Success in this claim would have allowed him to claim rights to all tithes arising from the sheep pastured on the commons as well as from all crops grown in temporary enclosure on the commons, potentially doubling or even tripling his tithes income (MacDermot 1973). The 1675 Map of Exmore (*see* Introduction) was produced in support of this case. His case failed, but the depositions of the witnesses provide valuable information about how the commons were viewed and used. First, it seems that the commons were widely cultivated. For instance, in 1678 Nicholas Snowe refers to paying tithes on corn and grain grown on the commons to the rectors of Exford and Porlock parishes. That this was not an unusual occurrence is supported by Nicholas Rawlinson's statement that 'for the last thirty five years to his knowledge parts of Exford Common have been ploughed up' (MacDermot 1973, 352). Similarly, George Gulley, 'Husbandman of Withepoole', stated that 'Part of the said [Withypoole] common has recently been tilled and there are signs that several other parts now laid down [to pasture] have been anciently tilled' (MacDermot 1973, 362).

Nineteenth-century authorities were also aware of this evidence for earlier reclamation. For instance, in 1851 Acland (1851, 32) noted that 'Some of the commons appear to have been in past times enclosed and abandoned, either because the soil was exhausted or the cultivation unprofitable'. Nearly 30 years later it was noted that 'There are certainly no traces of the Saxon plough on Exmoor, although the adjacent commons, now for the most part covered in heather, bear traces of having been enclosed and cultivated' (Sidney 1878, 75).

It is clear that for many years arable cultivation was seen as a normal use of the commons and went hand in hand with the pasture. This is reflected in the records of an early 17th-century dispute over the rights to the tithes of the commons. The defendants in this case stated that they had right of pasture on Monkham Common 'when the said commons lye fresh and are not in tillage'.

If Withypool and Hawkridge commons were typical, gaining permission from the lord of the manor to break up the commons seems to have been a relatively simple matter. In the 17th century all that was required was a payment of 4d or 6d per acre, 'the said payment never known to be denied' (MacDermot 1973, 351).

However, if the valuable pasture of the commons was to be reduced to produce crops, it must be productive. This was the real reason for the enclosure of the commons. For instance, in 1637, parts of Monkham Common had been cultivated for at least 60 years, the ploughed areas 'enclosed and fenced by a wall of earth and turfs and with frith and stakes for the preservation of the corn from sheep and cattle depasturing in the Forest' (MacDermot 1973, 293–4). Frith is composed of small branches or twigs and it was used to create 'dead-hedges' on the temporary intakes. The manorial courts kept a tight control over this dual use of the commons. For instance, in 1556 four men were instructed to make enclosures for cultivation on Almsworthy Common and in 1559 two farmers were fined because their cultivation of the common was not sufficiently protected by suitable hedges.

Exmoor's commons have been enclosed for outfield cultivation from at least the 13th century and probably earlier. In 1279 the inhabitants on the Somerset border complained that 'The Foresters attach … the men who work in their waste ground to make enclosures to sow corn, although the king has no demesne, the foresters attach these to come before them, and say that they have made waste and purprestre' (MacDermot 1973, 55).

Similarly, a 13th-century legal dispute in Devon between Forde Abbey and the Coffin family of Heanton, to the south-west of Lynton, indicates that arable cultivation and pasture did not always co-exist harmoniously. Both Forde Abbey as the 'lord of the soil', and the commoners, the Coffin family, had cultivated areas of the common at different times. However, the Coffins also strenuously fought to maintain their rights of pasture 'on the land after all the corn has been carried away and similar rights throughout the year on uncultivated land' (Gillard 2002, 190). That both parties had cultivated the waste would indicate that this was a temporary use of the commons as outfield. The Coffins later gave up their common rights for a fee of 40s, perhaps one of the earliest examples in Devon of enclosure by agreement (Gillard 2002).

Documentary evidence often refers to corn or oats being grown on the commons and it is likely that they were, but local tradition holds that rye was also cultivated. The remains of the fields are commonly referred to as 'rye banks' or 'rye beds' and anecdotal evidence suggests this arable tradition remained important well into the 19th century (Eardley-Wilmot 1990, 30; MacDermot 1973, 347). One 19th-century authority cites early, if somewhat circumstantial, evidence in support of an older date for rye cultivation on Exmoor:

> The 'undercoats' of the thatch of some of the oldest farmhouses, when pulled to pieces within living memory, were found to be of rye-straw, a crop which has not been grown in Somerset or North Devon in this or the previous century.
>
> (Sidney 1878, 75)

Recent analysis of the thatch of some of the older buildings on the Holnicote estate shows that they included rye among the oat and wheat straw which made up their base coats. Unfortunately this research has not yet provided an accurate date for their use (Daniel Bishop, pers comm; Letts 1991, 4–5).

Anecdotal evidence suggests that the method for cultivating rye on the commons was to plough the enclosed area and raise a contour bank below it so that heavy rain would not wash away the soil (Eardley-Wilmot 1990, 30). This was important as the soil on the commons was often shallow and of poor quality. Its productivity was often exhausted after only two or three crops, after which the enclosure was abandoned, the turf banks slowly crumbling and the commons reverting to pasture (MacDermot 1973, 8). The result is the patchwork of relict boundaries that survived as low earthworks on many of the commons well into the 20th century.

Enclosure in 18th and 19th centuries – potato gardens

In the 18th and 19th centuries, small potato gardens were enclosed by the tenants of the Holnicote estate on some of the eastern commons (Isabel Richardson, pers comm). Part of the Acland family's vast holdings, the Holnicote estate, controlled commons from Bossington, to the north-east of Porlock, to Dunkery Hill, and therefore had the power to grant their tenants the right to enclose land on a large number of Exmoor's commons.

The National Trust has carried out field surveys which have identified a number of small enclosures on the commons, such as those in Wychanger Combe. Their date and function was at first unknown, but documentary evidence dating from the 1760s to the 1870s has revealed their previously unrecognised role in the cultivation of the commons (Isabel Richardson, pers comm). For instance, a letter of 20 May 1769 from Sir T D Acland to James Willie of Steer's Cottage, Horner, discusses his right to enclose a piece of the 'Hill or Common called Horner Hill' for a potato plot no more than 0.4 hectares in size (DRO 1148 M add 2/67). Similar correspondence of 24 August 1772 discusses an application 'to take in and inclose with a good bank and quick-set hedge' 3 acres (1.2 hectares) of 'heathy ground' for a potato ground on 'Dunkry' or Dunkery Common, and 'to make a good ditch and bank around the three acres' (DRO 1148 M add 2/67). In 1820 Robert Buskin of Allerford wrote to Sir T D Acland requesting permission to cultivate 0.2 hectares for potatoes. The commons could be cultivated by anyone in this way on the payment of a small fee. In 1788 the Holnicote land agent's accounts list one year's rental of a potato garden on Wilmersham Common as 1s and the income from the rental of potato gardens in Bossington manor as 2s 6d (DRO 1148 M add. Agents Accounts Cridland).

These records not only shed light on how the commons were used but also give some hint of the motivation behind their cultivation. In 1810 Betty Elsworthy applied for a plot to grow potatoes on land in Allerford, possibly on Bossington Hill, because both her sons were away at sea (DRO 1148 M add 21/E1). In 1831 May Taylor of Dunster had 'paid ten shillings for potato ground and now the potatoes are taken by distress and then to be sold under the distress' (DRO 1148 M add 21/E1). It may be that the commons were cultivated for potatoes at times of unusual need.

Many of the known potato gardens around Holnicote are now obscured by later tree plantations, the majority of which were established by Sir T D Acland in the 19th century, a keen improver particularly committed to tree planting. Creating these plantations would have required him to relocate potato gardens already granted in those areas. For instance, at least seven potato gardens in Tivington plantation were relocated to a place called Peter's Ground (Isabel Richardson, pers comm, 20 May 2010).

Case study
Mill Hill and the coastal commons – rye banks and short-term enclosure

Mill Hill, part of Oare Common until its enclosure in 1862, is one of Exmoor's northern commons. It extends northwards, a long, finger-like spur, from the uplands of the royal forest. Although at less than 200 hectares it is not large in area, it is an imposing landform, rising steeply to nearly 400m above sea level from the deeply incised combes of Chalk Water to the west and Oare Water to the east.

Two episodes of enclosure are visible on its slopes. It is difficult to date relict field systems from earthwork evidence alone, but the earliest reclamation on Mill Hill could be medieval in date. Free from the constraints of forest law after disafforestment in the early 15th century, it is possible to imagine the commoners taking in field after field on

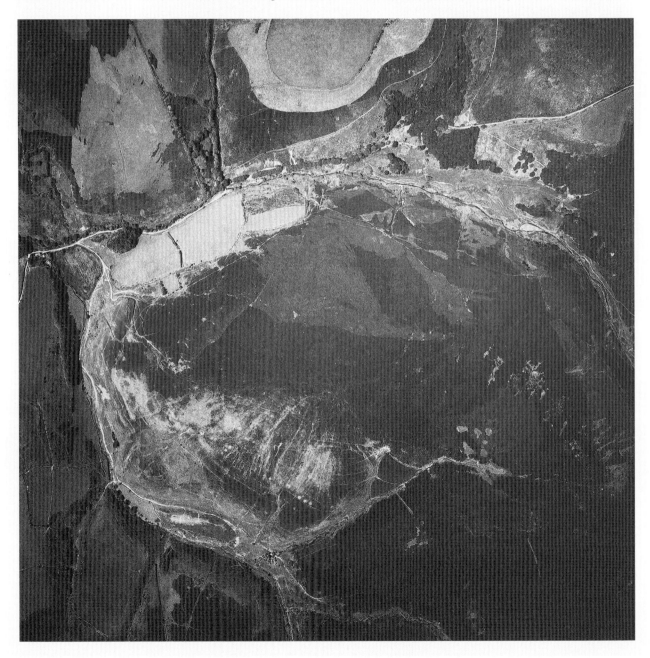

the sunnier south-west facing slopes above Chalk Water, enclosing first the steeper but lower gradients before climbing to the gentler but more exposed higher reaches of the common.

Some of the highest field enclosures appear to be unfinished and evidence of ploughing is scarce. Some areas of visible ridge and furrow are not enclosed. This could be evidence that the medieval cultivation of Mill Hill was short-lived and sporadic, or that ploughing was carried out as much to improve the pasture of the commons as for cultivation.

The enclosure of the north and eastern slopes of Mill Hill was probably later but proved, at least in part, more durable. Three large fields, currently used as pasture by Oareford Farm, are all that remain of a much larger field system. As many as eight further fields, similar in both form and elevation to those still in use, extended east and south above Weir Water, but had been abandoned by 1840. In the mid-19th century the remaining fields were used mostly for arable cultivation, only one-quarter turned over to pasture. By this time the rest of the common had reverted to rough pasture. Scars eroded into the hillside by rainwater running off the moor are now all that remain of the dividing banks between the abandoned fields.

The coastal common of Old Burrow Hill was, with the neighbouring Cosgate Hill and Hall Hill, part of the waste of Countisbury parish, extending from Countisbury in the west to County Gate in the east. Countisbury commons belonged to Forde Abbey from the 13th century until the Dissolution of the

Fig 2.20
Field systems on Mill Hill. Medieval enclosure has focused on the gentler south-west facing slopes, where irregular fields as well as ridge and furrow are visible. On the steeper northern slopes, a more organised – and perhaps later – system of fields has developed. On the steepest slopes the field banks and ditches have been eroded by rainwater running off the moor which has scoured out deep channels along the lines of the field boundaries.
[© John Hodgson]

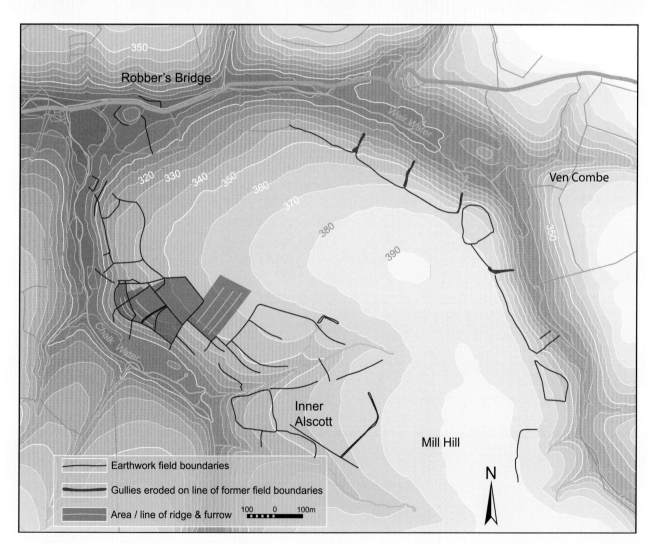

Robber's Bridge

Ven Combe

350

320 330 340 350 360 370 380 390

Weir Water

Chalk Water

Inner Alscott

Mill Hill

N

—— Earthwork field boundaries

—— Gullies eroded on line of former field boundaries

—— Area / line of ridge & furrow

100   0   100m

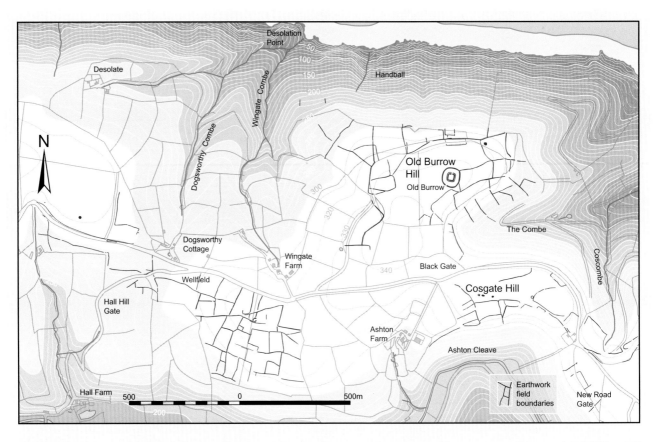

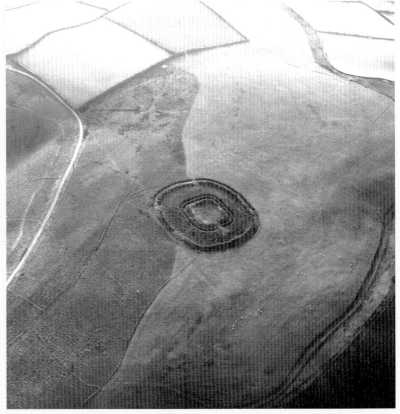

Fig 2.21 (above)
The dispersed pattern of farmsteads in Countisbury parish resulted in small pockets of common or waste lying between them. Some of these areas were enclosed in the 19th century and in the mid-20th century most remaining areas of heath were ploughed up. However, it is clear from aerial photographs that nearly all of these small commons were originally covered in field systems which appear to be medieval or post medieval in date. Over the summit of Cosgate Hill and south of Wingate Farm even the earlier line of the modern A39 coast road is visible preserved within the relict fields.
[© John Hodgson]

Fig 2.22 (right)
Traces of possibly medieval enclosure around Old Burrow Roman Fort remained visible into the second half of the 20th century.
[CUCAP (BAE97) 26-NOV-1969]

Fig 2.23 (left)
By the 1970s the location of the former enclosure fences were visible largely only as soilmarks, fragmentary earthworks surviving only on the steeper and more inaccessible slopes of the combe.
[OS/72065 (V) Frame 112 15-APR-1972 Lib 10332]

Fig 2.24 (below)
Medieval farmers reach the end of a long day reclaiming the coastal commons. The banks may have been built of turves, topped with a dead-hedge of stakes and frith. In the background, the sun sets over the earthworks of the Roman fort of Old Burrow.
[© John Hodgson]

Monasteries (1536–41) by Henry VIII. They were therefore probably cultivated and grazed in the medieval period in much the same way as the Abbey's other holdings in Lynton. As the boundary of the royal forest fluctuated, Old Burrow Common probably remained subject to forest law until the 15th century. The tithe map of 1839 shows Old Burrow Hill as rough pasture, free from any enclosure and it seems probable that the common was enclosed and reverted to pasture several times. Relict boundaries and faint traces of ridge and furrow recorded by aerial survey may represent only some of the phases of enclosure of the common. They represent a series of piecemeal intakes dating possibly to the 18th or early 19th century, although they may be older. Even slight earth-works can be surprisingly durable. Whatever the date, the enterprising commoners took advantage of the remains of the Roman fort, incorporating the ancient fortification into their field system.

Case study
Potato gardens

From the 1780s to the 1870s potato gardens must have been a familiar sight on the Holnicote estate commons. Tenants applied to the estate for permission to enclose and, if successful, paid around 1s for a year's rent for a patch of ground usually less than 1.2 hectares in area but often smaller than 0.4 hectares. In this way even a poor member of the parish could easily supplement their diet.

The gardens were usually made on the edge of the enclosed land, encroaching onto the commons in small, irregularly shaped plots. This piecemeal enclosure may have been cumulative, with one garden being attached to another. For example, in 1769 James Willie applied to enclose a patch on Horner Hill 'adjoining to J. Hill's potato plot' (DRO 1148M add 2/67).

Estate documents describe the enclosure of 1.2 hectares of 'heathy ground' for potato gardens on Dunkery Hill, 'on the right side of the highway leading from East Luccombe to Cloutsham'. This enclosure has not yet been identified.

In the early 19th century the 10th Baronet Acland 'improved' many of the Holnicote commons with tree planting, displacing many established potato gardens. Some relict enclosures survive within Middlehill and Horner plantations, and it is likely that more remain to be discovered in the surrounding plantations.

Adjacent to the ruins of Badgworthy Cottage are the ridges of a potato garden built by the shepherds who lived there in the 19th century; although now bracken covered, they can still be picked out on the ground in early spring.

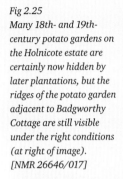

Fig 2.25
Many 18th- and 19th-century potato gardens on the Holnicote estate are certainly now hidden by later plantations, but the ridges of the potato garden adjacent to Badgworthy Cottage are still visible under the right conditions (at right of image). [NMR 26646/017]

The changing commons: landscapes of enclosure

> Since the beginning of the last century most of the moor has been legally if not physically enclosed, and the rights of common have consequently ceased save in one or two cases, but over a large area the actual fences are so few and far between as to make little difference in the aspect of the country.
>
> (MacDermot 1973, 10)

Enclosure is a very complex process. Economic and social historians have argued its causes and effects, amassing a vast body of literature in the process (for a concise introduction to the subject *see* Williamson 2000). On Exmoor, the recent NMP survey provides an opportunity to assess the impact of the enclosure process in shaping the landscape from an archaeological perspective.

Following the enclosure of the former royal forest, the wastes of the manorial commons remained the only unenclosed land on Exmoor available for improvement. As such, they became a resource under increasing pressure (Siraut 2009, 132). However, parliamentary enclosure came relatively late to Exmoor's commons. Although the open fields of the Midlands are arguably the best known examples, throughout England much of the parliamentary enclosure that took place between 1700 and 1870 concerned only common grazing. By 1836 around 728,500 hectares had been enclosed by acts dealing exclusively with commons, compared to half a million acres in the years after 1836 (Williamson 2002). Against this background, it is all the more surprising that it was 22 years after John Knight had purchased the forest before the Exmoor region was again affected by parliamentary enclosure. In 1841, a decade after its Act of Enclosure, Bratton Down and Berry Hill in Bratton Fleming parish to the west of Exmoor lost their commons to enclosure. The last enclosure on Exmoor was at Wootton Courtenay in 1872, some 18 years after its own Act (MacDermot 1973, 10).

However, parliamentary enclosure was not a unified process. Each enclosure required a separate act, usually proposed by the owner of the land. Each act therefore had its own agenda and this is often reflected in the way the commons were enclosed. In fact, the way the commons were perceived, both locally and nationally, changed dramatically between the first and last parliamentary enclosure on Exmoor. Indeed, the perception of enclosure changed to the extent that the Exmoor commons were some of the very last to be enclosed.

The earliest enclosures on Exmoor were probably private agreements, taking in the best unenclosed land remaining around anciently enclosed settlements. Late 18th-century enclosure by agreement took in some of the commons north of Challacombe, with further exchanges of land taking place in the 1840s. The regularity of the field system imposed on the commons by the 18th- and 19th-century surveyors is in stark contrast to the sinuous boundaries of medieval strip-fields, now fossilised in the field boundaries around the common edge (Riley and Wilson-North 2001, 99).

The enclosure of remaining commons around Challacombe and Parracombe in the 1860s prompted the Revd J F Chanter, Rector of Parracombe, to comment 'Now the moor can only be seen from this distance, the heather has disappeared, all has been fenced in, and wide roads have taken the place of the packhorse tracks' (Eardley-Wilmot 1990, 156). This may contrast with the view of the unenclosed commons expressed above by MacDermot, but in this we begin to see signs of the variety and complexity in the story of the enclosure of Exmoor's commons.

The enclosure of the commons

In the 18th and 19th centuries the commons came to be regarded by many not only as an obstacle to improvement, but as an active threat to society. Access to the resources of the commons allowed the poor too much independence and potentially attracted squatters, gypsies and other 'undesirables' (Williamson 2000, 72). It is probable that the earliest enclosure of Exmoor's commons had similar aims to the enclosure of the forest, where both economic and ideological factors influenced the decision to enclose. As with the royal forest, enclosure was a precursor to improvement, and the consolidation of land ownership, combined with the removal of common rights by enclosure, was necessary to allow agricultural reform.

Understandably commoners often took a different view. The resources of the commons were central to the operation of many farms, so much so that few new farms were created following the enclosure of the commons (Siraut 2009, 132).

Nonetheless, the established view that enclosure brought about the end of an old way of life and ruin to large sections of society is perhaps overemphasised. The loss of the commons certainly caused some hardship among the poor, particularly the very poor who relied on the natural resources of the commons for fuel or perhaps to keep small numbers of livestock or a few geese (Tarlow 2007). These landless inhabitants of the manor probably felt the loss of the commons most keenly. Without property and therefore no formal commons rights, they received no compensation when enclosure took place (Tarlow 2007, 47), and the provisions made for continuing access to the former common land were often meagre. This changed in 1845 when a General Parliamentary Act ensured that both commoners and the lord of the manor would receive a parcel of land in compensation for the loss of their rights (Clayden 2003, 3).

This could include allotments made in lieu of particular rights, as seen on the enclosure of Lyn Down in 1860 where the surveyor's allotments included the following provision:

> have set out and do hereby set out and allot and award unto the several Owners and Proprietors of Allotments under this Enclosure All that piece of parcel of land coloured red and numbered XV (15) on part 1 of the said map and containing by admeasurement Twenty acres three roods and nine perches to be in lieu of and in full compensation for all rights of turbary.

(DRO enclosure map 54)

Fig 2.26
The contrast between medieval piecemeal and post-medieval 'improvement-led' enclosure by agreement is strikingly illustrated by the Challacombe enclosure map. The map was created to record private exchanges of land in 1791, with the later 1859 enclosures annotated in red. [1261M/E22/20, courtesy of Devon Heritage Centre]

In general, however, the loss of access to the commons, particularly for the poor of the parish, was compensated for by the provision of a small area of land for communal use. Some areas of land were set aside for quarries, while others were allotted to the 'churchwardens and overseers of the Poor … to be held by them and their successors in trust as an allotment for the Labouring Poor' (DRO Map 64). This could be used as the parish saw fit, for grazing, the gathering or cutting of fuel, or even the provision of a poorhouse. In seemingly generous gestures, portions of land were even left open as so-called pleasure grounds for the inhabitants of the parish (Riley and Wilson-North 2001, 127). In reality these were no great concessions. Out of 25,000 hectares enclosed from 1845 to 1865,

only 1,600 hectares were allotted for the benefit of the poor (Clayden 2003, 3). Perceptions were beginning to shift against enclosure and, as at Withypool Common, petitions for overgreedy enclosure were being rejected (MacDermot 1973; Mold 1992).

Canny enclosers had, therefore, to be seen to make some redress on enclosure – no matter how paltry. For example, on the enclosure of Kentisbury Down – an area of around 190 hectares – the surveyor magnanimously stated:

I … do hereby set out and allot and award unto the churchwardens and overseers of the Poor of the said parish of Kentisbury all that piece or parcel of land numbered 42 on the map A containing three acres and eight

Fig 2.27
From the open land of
Challacombe Common,
we can look south past the
regular and straight sided
fields of 18th-century
enclosure to the sinuous
and irregular fields on
the northern edge of the
medieval hamlet.
[NMR 18323/05 SS6842/5
27-APR-1999]

Poles to be held by them and their successors in trust as a place of exercise and recreation for the inhabitants of the said Parish and Neighbourhood.

(DRO enclosure map 49)

In actuality allotments of 3 or 4 acres (1.5 hectares) were of little practical use and were often neglected. An inquiry of 1910 found that the Parracombe pleasure-ground was 'not used for any purpose and is quite unproductive', and

it remained unenclosed but unused thereafter (Mold 1992).

However, by the 19th century those who wholly relied on the commons for their living were probably very few. It was possibly the small farmers who suffered the greatest losses. Parliamentary enclosure was usually led by large landowners with the financial means to cover the costs of enclosing a common. Legal expenses aside, it could cost up to £40 to enclose a 4 hectare field, costs which would have been

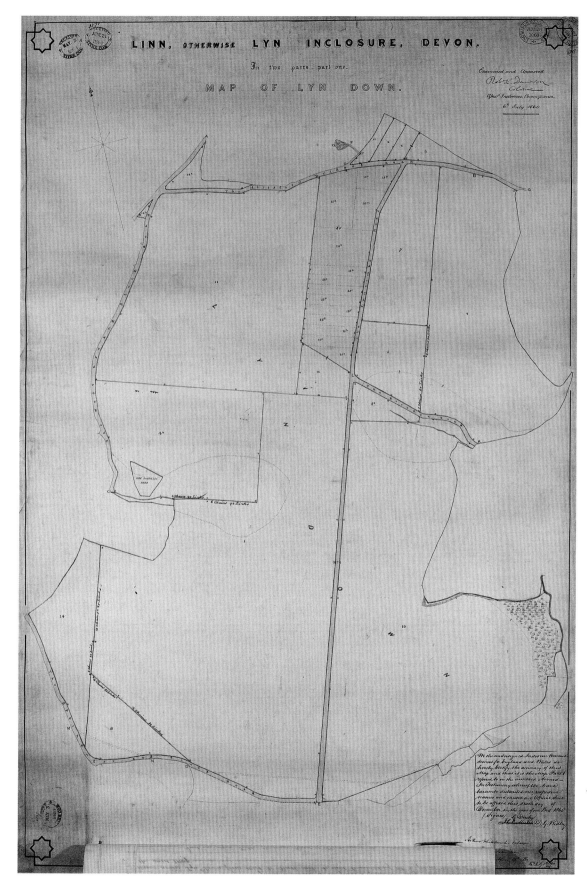

*Fig 2.28
On Lyn Down,
the enclosure
surveyor set
aside a small
area of land,
marked in red,
as compensation
for the commoners'
loss of rights of
turbary.
[DRO enclosure
map 54 Courtesy
of Devon Heritage
Centre]*

Fig 2.29 (below)
The south-west corner of
Lyn Down, where three
phases of landscape history
meet: 19th-century
enclosure fences meet
medieval boundaries, one
of which in turn encloses
the Iron Age hillslope
enclosure of Stock Castle.
[© Devon County Council]

Fig 2.30 (facing page)
Plot 42 (highlighted), an
area of just over 1.2 hectares
out of a total of 190 hectares
of Kentisbury Down was set
aside 'as a place of exercise
and recreation' for the former
commoners of the parish.
[Courtesy of Devon Heritage
Centre]

beyond the means of many smaller farmers. Often it was simply more practical to sell their apportionments (Acland and Sturge 1851, 27; Siraut 2009, 132).

It is true that 'a new pattern of life had to be devised' (Eardley-Wilmot 1990), but enclosure itself cannot be blamed for the hardships which followed. Instead, enclosure should really be seen as the logical conclusion of the ongoing process of farm engrossment and ever-increasing farm size, a process that was occurring throughout England (Williamson 2002, 74). On Exmoor by the 1880s medium-sized farms of up to 120 hectares were being lost in Exford, Hawkridge and Winsford, as large farms 320 hectares or more in size were being created, such as South Court, Wellshead and Stone (Siraut 2009, 134). In this environment, enclosure actually brought those landowners and farmers who could afford enclosure a great many more advantages than disadvantages, such as improved communications, more compact and easily managed farmsteads and longer leases (Tarlow 2007, 47).

The end of parliamentary enclosure

By the end of the 1860s things were beginning to change. A number of factors conspired to make the enclosure of commons less attractive. Cheap imports of corn from America curbed the economic urge to turn commons over to arable cultivation, while increasing industrialisation increased the perception of commons as important places for recreation (Clayden 2003, 3).

An important turning point was the creation in 1865 of the Commons Preservation Society, now more commonly called the Open Spaces Society. Originally founded to prevent the enclosure of commons in the south-east of England, this society was instrumental in establishing

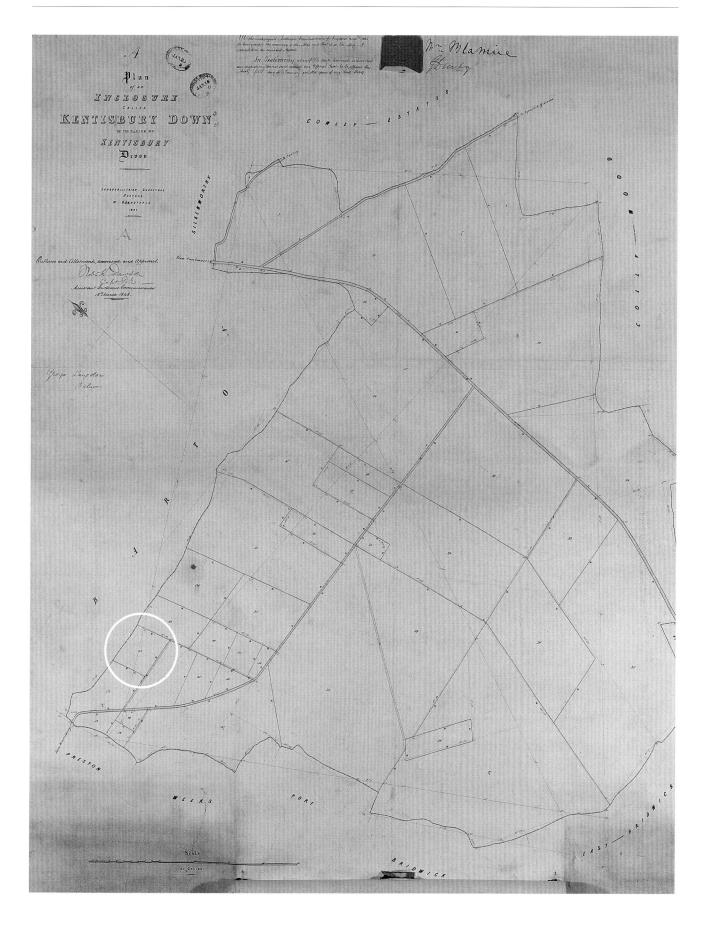

Fig 2.31 (above)
The angularity of the
Kentisbury Down enclosure
boundaries direct the gaze
past the surrounding
anciently enclosed land
towards the remaining
unenclosed coastal commons
and heaths of Holdstone
and Trentishoe Down,
bounded by the sharply
incised combes of
Sherrycome to the west and
Heddon's Mouth to the east.
[NMR 26643/037 (UNCAT)
18-AUG-2009]

Fig 2.32 (right)
'… not used for any purpose
and is quite unproductive' –
the damning verdict on the
value of the 'pleasure
ground' on Parracombe
Common.
[Courtesy Exmoor National
Park Authority]

THE COMMON A-TOOK IN

Oh! No, Poll, no! Since they've a-took

The common in, our lew wold nook

Don't seem a-bit as used to look

When we had runnèn room;

Girt banks do shut up ev'ry drong,

An stratch wi' thorny backs along,

Where we did used to run among

The vuzzen an' the broom.

Ees; while the ragged colt did crop

The nibbled grass, I used to hop

The emmet-buts, vrom top to top,

So proud o' my spry jumps:

Wi' thee beside or at my zide,

A-skippèn on so light an' wide

'S thy little frock would let thes stride,

Among the vuzzy humps.

Ah while the lark up over head

Did twitter, I did search the red

Thick bunch o' broom, or yollow bed

O' vuzzen for a nest;

An thou di'st hunt about, to meet

Wi strawberries so red an' sweet

Or wild thyme vor thy breast;

Or when the cows did run about

A-stung, in zummer, by the stout,

Or when they play'd, or when they fought,

D'ist stand a-lookèn on:

An' where white geese, wi' long red bills,

Did veed among the emmet hills,

There we did goo to vind their quills

Alongzide o' the pon.

What fun there wer among us, when

The Hayward come, wi' all his men,

To drève the common, an' to pen

Strange cattle in the pound:

The cows did bleäre, the men did shout

An toss the eärms an' stick's about,

An vo'ks, to own their stock came out,

Vrom all the housen round.

(Barnes, William 1888)

the legal framework which now governs the way commons are managed nationwide, influencing the enactment of early legislation such as the Metropolitan Commons Act 1866 and the Commons Acts 1876 and 1899. Through such acts, the commons were increasingly perceived as important breathing spaces, to be cherished for their amenity value rather than their agricultural potential (Clayden 2003, 3; Winchester 2006, 14).

This is clearly illustrated on Withypool Common. Enclosure at Withypool was first mooted in the annual Bill for the Enclosure Commissioners of 1869. Only one of the 1,800 acres to be enclosed was set aside for the leisure use of the inhabitants and the enclosure was rejected out of hand. A second attempt in 1879 set aside 4.25 hectares but this too was rejected, the enclosure now viewed as not providing any 'public advantage' (MacDermot 1973, 11).

Although the commons legislation was originally developed to save the village greens and lowland heaths of south-eastern England rather than the upland commons of hill farming districts such as Exmoor, it reflected the changing perceptions of commons and undoubtedly also included such areas (Winchester 2006, 14). Increasing focus on the amenity value of upland commons in the early 20th century directly encouraged the development of the National Parks movement and, ultimately, the creation of Exmoor National Park in 1954, of which the commons today remain a small but intrinsic and highly significant part.

The commons continue to contribute to the special qualities of the National Park – its character, historic environment and wildlife – and if they are to continue to do so, they must overcome a number of challenges shared, to a greater or lesser degree, by commons all over the country.

The heritage of the commons is of national significance. Over centuries their management has created landscapes of rich natural and archaeological value, with 20 per cent now within Sites of Special Scientific Interest and 11 per cent of England's nationally important scheduled monuments associated with common land. Of the 7,000 or so commons registered in England today, over 75 per cent fall either within a National Park (48 per cent) or an Area of Outstanding Natural Beauty (30 per cent). Of these, 21 are within Exmoor National Park.

However, both on Exmoor and nationally, the future of the commons is uncertain. Even

Case study
Parliamentary enclosure of the commons – the holding of Holdstone Down

Holdstone Down, formerly part of the commons of Combe Martin, is an imposing and exposed landscape. The oval hill rises sharply to a height of nearly 350m from steep sea cliffs to the north, and to the west the down drops dramatically into the steep valley of Sherrycombe. In places the underlying geology gives the down the appearance of a series of stepped terraces, clearly visible on aerial photographs. To the east lies the parish of Trentishoe and the unenclosed slopes of Trentishoe Down.

Several phases of early enclosure encircle the lower slopes of the hill, probably expanding over time from the surrounding farmsteads. By the medieval period the downs provided the inhabitants of Combe Martin with common land where they exercised their rights of turbary and pasture.

Enclosure came to Combe Martin in the 19th century. However, the enclosure of Holdstone Down was a rare instance of the process being subverted by the commoners for their own ends. To this day much of the down still appears to be unenclosed moorland. In fact, Holdstone Down is the most subdivided area of land on Exmoor. In 1871 the downs were divided into 270 individual strips or plots, each one allotted to a commoner. The contrast between this and the classic enclosure as seen at Kentisbury Down could not be more striking. This division was intentional and reflected growing discontent with the inequalities of enclosure. The enclosure surveyor's closing statement explains that 'the persons to

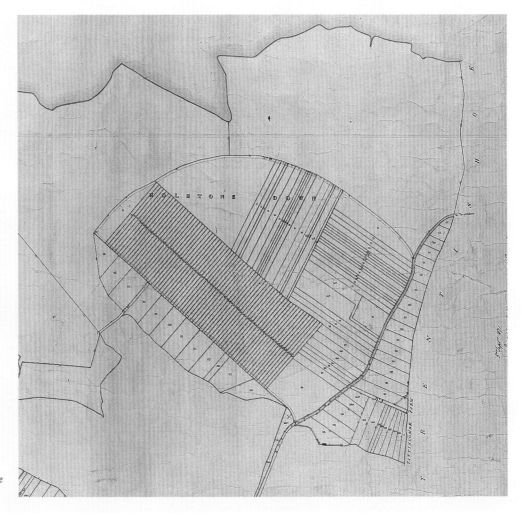

Fig 2.33
By taking enclosure to the extreme and intermixing their allotted portions of the down, the commoners of Holdstone Down, part of Combe Martin parish, frustrated the process of parliamentary enclosure. [Courtesy of Devon Heritage Centre]

whom the allotments ... are allotted have given notice in writing that they desire to have their allotments thrown together and distinguished by metes and bounds but not fenced from each other' (DRO Map 25). By intermixing their allotments in this way, the commoners turned the process of enclosure to their advantage, frustrating the goals of those who saw enclosure as a means to deny common rights (Riley and Wilson-North 2001). Consequently much of the down remains unenclosed to the present day, the corners of the individual allotments instead being marked with numbered boundary stones. Each numbered stone can be correlated with a numbered strip on the enclosure map, and thence to the enclosure award and the name of the individual commoner to whom the strip was allotted.

In this way the commoners effectively kept their common unenclosed, retaining the down for their traditional rights, although a few attempted to grow potatoes there (Beaumont 1989). On Holdstone Down, instead of improved pasture and straight-edged boundaries, the legacy of enclosure is the wild heather that grows on the down itself and the few remaining stones that lurk among the moorland vegetation.

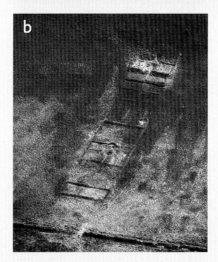

Fig 2.34 (above left)
Instead of fencing their allotments, each plot was 'distinguished by metes and bounds' or marker stones, individually numbered to tally with the divisions marked on the enclosure map. In this way the commoners retained access to the pasture of the down.
[Courtesy of Hazel Riley]

Fig 2.35a and b
To offset the cost of enclosure, part of the down was sold off to a private buyer and in the 1890s a grandiose plan was drawn up to build a holiday village on the northern fringes of the down. On the sale plan, plots were laid out along a road known as 'Sea View Road' (Beaumont 1989), while a spur led away from it along 'Beach Road'. Sea View Road survives as a trackway (now part of the South West Coast Path), while Beach Road, if built, would have had to negotiate the near vertical sea cliffs on the 350m descent to the foreshore. The scheme seems, therefore, to have been disingenuous at best! Nevertheless 50 of the original 143 plots were sold. Today 'villas' occupy only two plots, but the other less successful developments can be traced among the gorse bushes and bracken.
[(a) NMR 21074/30 SS6247/13 09-FEB-2001; (b) NMR 26643/005 [UNCAT] 18-AUG-2009]

Fig 2.36
The feral goats in the Valley
of Rocks near Lynton may
be a draw for tourists but
they can present a challenge
in managing the common,
as well as a threat to the
flowerbeds and allotments
of local residents.
[© Rob Wilson-North]

through agreements with landowners, or the consolidation of ownership bringing the ownership and all the rights of common under a single estate, the land thereby technically ceasing to be a common. In such a complex situation the effective management of the commons is of increasing importance. The widespread reclamation of unimproved moorland commons is now clearly undesirable, both from an ecological and archaeological point of view. However, to effectively manage them presents practical and economic challenges.

Only a handful of Exmoor's commons remain in use as a central part of an upland farming regime, with a small number of commoners or graziers actively managing their commons. Some, such as Brendon and Withypool are managed by active and self-regulating commoners associations. However, problems of access and stock management make others, such as the coastal commons and heaths, difficult to graze effectively, often exacerbated by individual peculiarities such as the presence of feral goats in the Valley of Rocks near Lynton. Unfortunately, in the absence of overseeing bodies, such as commoners associations or the old manorial courts, other commons have been subject to unregulated and inconsiderate stocking, dissuading other commoners from using and therefore maintaining this valuable resource.

the definition of what comprises common land remains complex. Owing to the rushed nature of the Commons Registration Act 1965, land commonly perceived and used as a common may in fact not be legally registered as such. Even if it is, it may not have any active or registered commoners managing the land.

In addition, an increasing number of commons are disappearing. A number of factors can cause this to happen, such as the remaining commoners giving up their common rights

Fig 2.37
Commoners rounding up
Exmoor ponies at
Weatherslade, Withypool.
[© Chris Chapman]

Section 3

The farmland

Farming and the farmstead

The farm is the lifeblood of this landscape. From the medieval period onwards the farm, and farmstead at its heart, have driven 'improvements' to the surrounding land. Changes in farming practice reflect wider developments in society, technology or the ideology of farming, and can be read at the farm scale. It is these changes that underpin the fundamental character of the landscape today and chart the fortunes of individual farms and farming practice across the last seven centuries.

The settlement pattern on and around Exmoor is complex, but is dispersed in character (Riley and Wilson-North 2001, 92; Siraut 2009, 78). There are a few nucleated villages, a number of hamlets and over 600 individual farms. Many parishes can trace the modern settlement pattern directly to that of 14th-century farmsteads, via lay subsidy returns, which provide lists of taxpayers often with locative surnames (Aston 1983).

Exmoor farms tend to be on these ancient sites, but this is not to say that settlement is static or unchanging. The group of buildings

Fig 3.1
Silcombe Farm occupies a combe head location, and has been occupied since medieval times. In the 19th century a new farmhouse was built and a planned farmstead around a courtyard. The site of the old farm is represented by earthworks in the field below.
[NMR 18530/19 SS8348/9 12-OCT-1999]

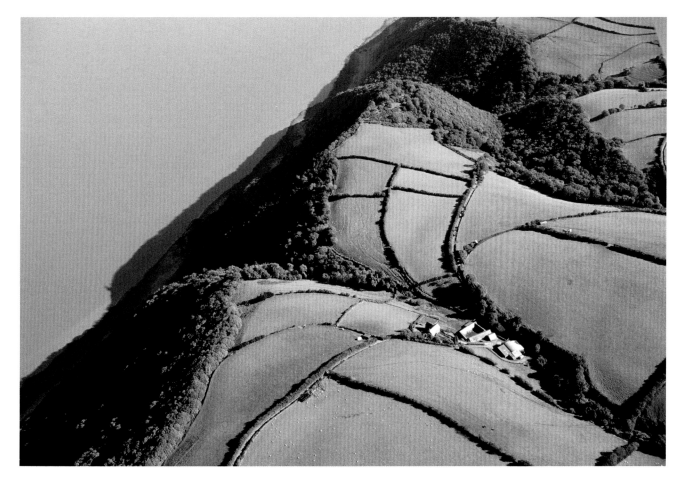

101

Fig 3.2

At Sweetworthy where enclosed farmland meets the moorland mass of Dunkery, are the remains of several prehistoric enclosed settlements (top left) and the earthworks of a deserted medieval settlement (in the gorse at the centre of the photograph). Such instances of apparent and demonstrable continuity from prehistoric times to the medieval period are rare on Exmoor. [23826/23]

that forms the farmstead typically comprises a post-medieval farmhouse, perhaps dating from the 17th century, surrounded by a collection of farm buildings which are nearly always Victorian.

From the 11th to the 14th centuries Exmoor, in common with much of England, enjoyed a period of favourable climate, improved agriculture and an expanding population. With little land available for expansion, farmsteads became subdivided, resulting in the creation of paired farms such as East and West Nethercote in Winsford (Siraut 2009, 58). This practice continued, sporadically, into the 18th century, with many farms being divided and settlements evolving into hamlets of two, three or even more farms or smallholdings. For instance, at Swincombe in Challacombe parish, the hamlet still comprises the farms of North Swincombe, West Swincombe Farm, Little Swincombe Farm and South Swincombe. In Hartland, north Devon, some hamlets contained as many as 10

holdings and it is likely that settlement patterns on the fringes of Exmoor were as dense (Fox 1983, 40). Hamlets were so numerous that they were almost certainly the dominant form of settlement on Exmoor during the medieval period although individual farms continued to exist (Riley and Wilson-North 2001, 92–3).

The 14th to 17th centuries saw climatic deterioration and poor harvests, with perhaps one-third of England's population lost to plague (Siraut 2009, 63). During this period even isolated parishes saw a dramatic drop in numbers and changes to their settlement structure. For instance, in Hartland between 1301 and 1566 nine hamlets became completely deserted (Fox 1983, 40). However, the extreme inaccessibility of many of Exmoor's settlements may have protected them from the worst ravages of disease. For instance, of the 49 settlements in existence in Brushford, Dulverton, Molland and Winsford in 1327, only five had been deserted by the 19th century, although some farms may have shifted or continued under different names (Siraut 2009, 64). Of the desertions which did occur, climatic change was probably the major factor in abandonment, perhaps in favour of farms made available by disease in the lowlands (Riley and Wilson-North 2001, 95). Only five significant desertions have been recorded, at Badgworthy, Mansley Combe, Ley Hill, Grexy Combe and Sweetworthy, and the available dating evidence suggests that abandonment occurred between the 15th and 16th centuries (Riley and Wilson-North 2001, 93–4).

The occurrence of only a few medieval desertions on Exmoor indicates that many settlement sites continue to the present, and have been altered so much over time that the archaeological evidence for medieval occupation is elusive.

Settlement contraction or amalgamation, as opposed to complete abandonment, appears to have been more common. It points towards a dynamic and responsive settlement form, which has a built-in flexibility and consequently an ability to endure the hardships of life in the uplands, but how these settlements adapted and evolved is still poorly understood. Around Lyshwell, a predominantly 19th-century farmstead on the edge of Molland Moor, are five deserted farmsteads (one of which was built in the 19th century), which may have previously formed a hamlet. The evolution of this settlement to a single farmstead is clearly one of engrossment, but the detailed process is far from clear (Riley and Wilson-North 2001, 130–1). At Higher Holwell in Parracombe are the earthworks of an abandoned medieval hamlet. However, Holwell was one of many townships which, although independent in development, formed the dispersed core of the wider village of Parracombe (Riley and Wilson-North 2001, 117). Although the reasons for its desertion are unclear, the earthworks should perhaps more accurately be read as a contraction or

Fig 3.3
At Higher Holwell, the earthworks of a deserted hamlet, trackways, fields, and ridge and furrow are best interpreted as part of the contraction and evolution of Parracombe village rather than a complete abandonment. [DAP LC09 10-JAN-1989 Frances Griffith © Devon County Council]

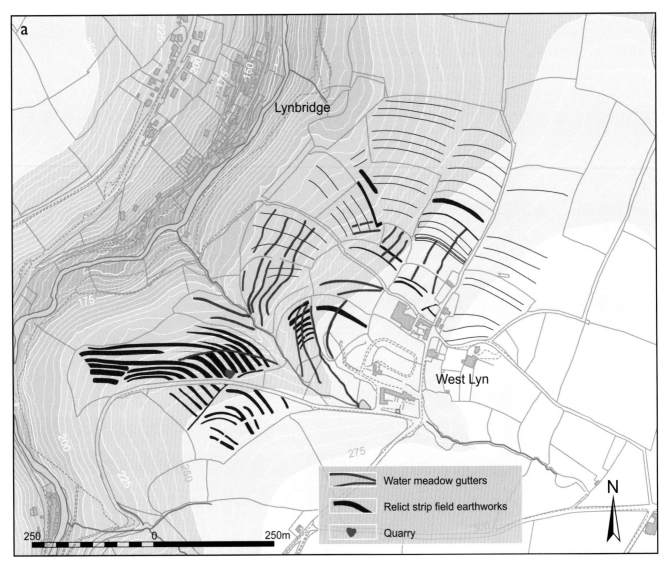

Lynbridge

West Lyn

Water meadow gutters

Relict strip field earthworks

Quarry

250   0   250m

N

Fig 3.4a and b
Fossilised medieval strip
fields at West Lyn. Note the
later, possibly 19th-century,
water meadow cutting the
earlier field boundaries.
[(a, above) © John Hodgson;
(b, facing page) © Cambridge
University copyright
reserved. ENPA CUCAP
(Zki-FD 51 2) 02-NOV-
1995]

consolidation of the main settlement, rather than a single desertion.

Documentary research has shown that many of today's farms came into being through a series of expansions and contractions, or simply a change of settlement focus. However, this process is generally more difficult to identify archaeologically than that of settlement or farm desertion (Aston 1983, 1999; Fox 1983, 41). With desertion, earthworks or ruined structures remain to indicate the former farmstead, but as hamlets contract, tenants might be persuaded to take on the abandoned holdings. However, it would be uneconomical for either tenant or lord of the manor to also maintain surplus farmsteads and outbuildings. At Stoke Fleming in South Devon the 1468 court rolls record that 'John Foterel takes three holdings from the lord yet need repair and sustain [only] a hall, a bake-

house and a barn' (Fox 1983, 41; DRO 902M/ M22, Court Rolls Manor of Stoke Fleming 1467– 1468). Some farm buildings might be incorporated into the new holding, but others would be abandoned or removed 'so that a hamlet grouping of farmsteads around a small green would eventually become a deceptively simple collection of outbuildings around a spacious farmyard' (Fox 1983, 42).

The process of engrossment is difficult but not impossible to see, and can be reflected in the wider landscape around the farmstead. Earthwork remains of formerly extensive strip fields cluster around the hamlets within the parishes of Parracombe and Challacombe. These remains have been interpreted as evidence of former open fields, cultivated in common by the inhabitants of each hamlet (Riley and Wilson-North 2001, 99). Strip fields recorded in West Lyn, near Lynton

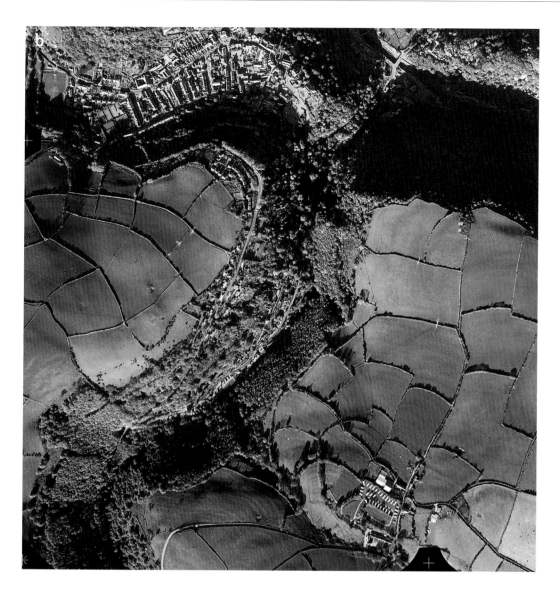

and Lynmouth, are of similar complexity, however, significant differences between the remains exist. Whereas the relict Parracombe and Challacombe strip fields often remain associated with a number of farms forming small hamlets, the majority of the West Lyn strip fields are now within the single holding of West Lyn Farm.

During the medieval period the strip fields would have formed the communal arable infield for several farms and smallholdings. The extent of this infield is discernible today, crystallised in several long curving boundaries to the west of West Lyn Farm. However, probably from the 14th century onwards, the pattern of land use began to change towards a pastoral economy and the arable infield converted to pasture. Within the extant field boundaries we can see fossilised the end result of potentially hundreds of years of piecemeal enclosure, a long process of amalga-

mation as parcels of land were exchanged and enclosed as land ownership increasingly became concentrated into fewer and fewer hands (Berry 2003). As late as 1840 the land comprising West Lyn Farm was divided between four owners and six tenants, including at least two farms, West Lyn farm and North Town farm, the name of which may highlight West Lyn's township past (Riley and Wilson-North 2001, 117).

It is likely that amalgamation was caused by several factors. First, years of agricultural innovation had improved the efficiency of farming; second, enclosure and the loss of common land and rights had made smaller holdings less viable; third, the agricultural depression of the late 19th century forced less economic farms to fail. This period saw the greatest number of farm desertions and amalgamations on Exmoor (Siraut 2009, 116).

Case study
North Thorne – a deserted medieval settlement and its fields

At North Thorne near Bratton Fleming are the traces of two medieval houses and several holloways forming the core of a small hamlet. The settlement was probably deserted in the early 14th century, and now survives as earthworks in a field a few hundred metres to the south-east of the modern North Thorne Farm (Brooks, 1992; Hurst and Wilson, 1962). As at West Lyn and Challacombe, existing hedges fossilise the line of the former infield around the deserted hamlet. Beyond, the character of enclosure changes dramatically: the straight and regular field boundaries associated with North Thorne farm dominate and are clearly imposed onto the medieval strip fields. Such a wholesale reorganisation of the farming landscape would only have been possible if these strip fields were completely out of use.

This was not the end of the story, for in the 1950s, Wistlanpound Reservoir was built, and by the 1970s further improvements meant that the traces of the strip fields had been effaced.

Fig 3.5a and b
Aerial photographs from the 1940s and 1970s reveal the traces of the relict medieval landscape at North Thorne and chart the development of the landscape through the 20th century.
[(a) NMR RAF CPE/ UK/2082 3096 19-MAY-1947; (b) NMR OS/73109 911 29-APR-1973]

Fig 3.6
A typical hillside catch
meadow on Exmoor in Long
Combe near Larkbarrow.
[© Rob Wilson-North]

Water and the farm

He that doth drown is a good husband.
(Hereford proverb, Kerridge 1973, 111)

Water is the lifeblood of any farm and water management a key part of farming life. With too little water, crops wither and livestock perish; with too much, land can lie stagnant, boggy and unproductive. Drainage and irrigation, therefore, became vital activities on the farm and can be seen as two sides of the same coin.

I would here venture a remark, that many thousand acres of hill-side land are now lying waste … which might be profitably brought into good cultivation by the aid of capital, enterprise and good water … This done, it would serve as a key to the whole occupation, by affording abundance of hay for the winter season, early feed for the ewes and lambs and, what is best, little manure need be returned to the meadow.
(Smith 1851, 147–8)

Water management was carefully integrated into the fabric of the farmstead. This often began with tapping a moorland stream, feeding it via a leat through the farmstead – both to bring water to the buildings, to provide power and to carry effluent away – and ended with the irrigation of the hillsides and combe slopes of the infield pasture.

Farm-scale artificial irrigation, or 'floating' as it is often called, used water meadows to apply water to the pasture, a process that is traditionally known as 'drowning'. The intention of such irrigation was to improve the productivity of the ground, which was of great benefit in hill farming regions.

Generally speaking, two types of water meadow are known in England. Possibly the best known are called bedworks, and comprise elaborate systems of earthwork channels, sluices and dams, which were used to irrigate the floors of the broad river valleys of much of southern England. These developed probably between the 17th and 19th centuries and most commonly were used in the chalk valleys of Wessex, but were also installed in other, less appropriate environments by over-enthusiastic improvers (Wade-Martins and Williamson 1999; Williamson and Cook 2003).

The second type of water meadow is known variously as the field gutter system, catchwork or, as they will be called here, the catch meadow. Catch meadows probably predate bedworks; they were also more widely distributed, used throughout Britain from East Anglia to the north of Scotland, and even recorded throughout much of mainland Europe from Scandinavia to Italy (Taylor 2007; Taylor *et al* 2006). In England, however, catch meadow irrigation was most widespread in the western counties of Somerset, Devon and Cornwall, and was concentrated in the narrow and sharply incised combes of Exmoor, so that by the end of the 19th century virtually every farm on Exmoor had a catchwork meadow system.

The significance of catch meadows

For many years there was little interest in the archaeology of water meadows, and what early work did take place was sometimes 'misguided and confused' (Taylor 2007, 23). However, in recent years this subject has received increasing attention, and its importance to farming has been fully realised (for an overview see Cook and Williamson 2007).

A number of recent works cite Exmoor's catch meadows as a remarkable application of this method of irrigation, but many have focused solely on those catch meadows constructed within the former royal forest after enclosure, perhaps because they were so well publicised at the time (Acland and Sturge 1851; Bettey 1999; Cook 1994; Smith 1851, 1856; Taylor 2007). Read in isolation, their somewhat evangelical reports could be taken to imply that catch meadows were introduced to Exmoor only after the enclosure of the former

royal forest and that they are a 19th-century development.

Roughly contemporary accounts of catch meadow away from the former royal forest, such as Roals' 1845 account of 'converting a moory hillside into Catch Meadow', extend the distribution slightly but reinforce the 19th-century focus. Field survey at Larkbarrow Farm in the former royal forest (Jamieson 2001, 2003) has greatly improved understanding of catch meadow operation; similarly, a study of Cloggs Farm, Withypool and Hawkridge (Brown 2005), has gone some way to dispel the bias towards the 19th-century farms of the former royal forest. But studies of individual sites, no matter how valuable, can do little to improve the appreciation of their true distribution.

In 1984 a far-sighted and innovative attempt was made to identify the distribution of catch meadows throughout the National Park from aerial photographs (Francis 1984). However, it is only as a result of thorough and comprehensive aerial survey that the true distribution of catch meadows around Exmoor has been revealed. Not only can it be shown that almost every farm had a catch meadow, but their operation can be

Fig 3.7
The distribution of catch meadows on and around Exmoor.
[© John Hodgson]

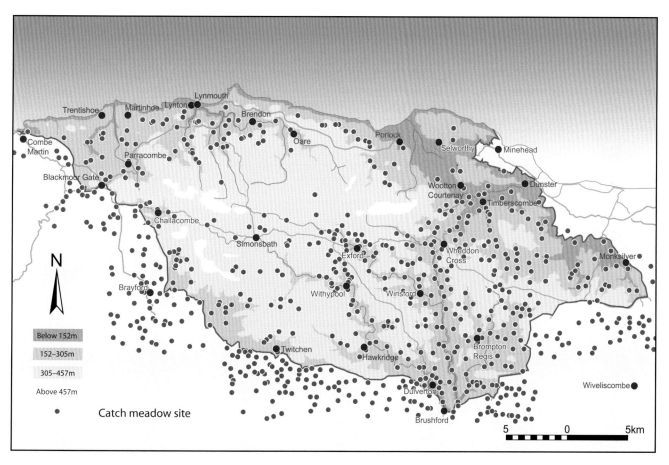

assessed. In total over 800 catch meadows were newly recorded from aerial photographs (Hegarty and Toms 2009; H Winton, pers comm).

Farming improvements, fertilisers and mechanisation in the 20th century meant that many of Exmoor's catch meadows not only passed out of use but were often deliberately levelled. This process is recorded in the aerial photographs taken since the Second World War, which have now become a valuable record of past landscapes and a primary source for identifying the former location of these transient features.

The origins of catch meadows

The antiquity of catch-meadow irrigation is largely unappreciated. When the water meadows of Exmoor are discussed it is often in terms only of those created on the former royal forest following enclosure. For instance, they have been described as being part of a rare 'hay production system' established as part of a 'grandiose reclamation scheme' (Wade Martins and Williams 1994, 36) and confidently asserted that 'Here, these systems only date from the early nineteenth century' (Cook 1994, 61). Such descriptions are correct as far as they go, that is, as far as the boundary of the former royal forest.

However, the origin and development of 'drowning' or 'floating' remains a much debated subject, and these 19th-century improvements should be viewed in the correct historic context (Cook and Williamson 2007; Cook *et al* 2003; Taylor *et al* 2006).

The *General Views of Agriculture* for the counties of Somerset and Devon describes catch meadows in operation in 1798 and 1808. Writing of Somerset, Billingsley (1794, 264) stated that:

the *watered meadows* in the parishes of Crowcombe, Stogumber, Monksilver, Nettlecomb, Dinnington, Dunster, Dulverton &c are as good as any in the county. If we appreciate land by its capacity for keeping stock throughout the year, watered meadows are invaluable.

Clearly describing catch meadows, he continues:

A great part of the watered lands lie on steep declivities; and as the water passes quickly over them, and never lies stagnant, not a rush can be seen.

Vancouver (1808, 314–5) paints a similar picture in Devon, where

The practice obtains very generally through most of the vallies in the county and where the land has been previously drained, and in proper preparation, it seldom fails to answer very fully the expectations of the farmer.

While uncomplimentary about much of the agricultural practice he saw in the county, William Marshall, wrote that the efficacy of the catch meadows of Devon were almost on a par with those of the chalk hills of Wiltshire and Hampshire (Marshall 1796, 208). So it is clear that catch meadows were well established in the hinterlands of Exmoor by the late 18th century.

A map of Halberton, to the north-east of Tiverton, created in 1603–8 to illustrate evidence in a dispute over water rights, graphically illustrates the importance and extent of water management in Devon's early 17th-century landscape (Turner 2007, 84; DRO 6065Z). In his *Synopsis Chorographical of Devonshire*, the Devon antiquary and civic leader John Hooker described the agricultural practices of Devonshire farmers, including water management:

if theire growndes be higher then theire greatest industrie is howe to conveye some runninge streame of water into it: wch if they do carie it throughe some wayes the same is the fatter and better wth the shoures and raynes: but if the waters be standinge pooles and a hungrye water they do amende the same by castinge of donge and lyme into it and this they do sturre with a staffe and so carye it throughe the growndes and medowes.

(Blake 1915, 344)

Although completed in 1600, Hooker's description of catch meadow irrigation must describe activities customary earlier in the 16th century.

Elsewhere in England, Rowland Vaughan published a work entitled 'Most Approved and Long Experienced Water-Workes' in 1610, in which he describes a method of irrigation applied to his Golden Valley estate on the banks of the River Dore in Herefordshire in the 1580s. His account was, however, 'ponderous, pompous, repetitive, verbose and in many places totally incomprehensible' (Taylor *et al* 2006, 38). Vaughan dedicated his volume to William,

22nd earl of Pembroke, whose Wiltshire estates contain bedworks dated at least from the 1630s. The confusion of his accounts and this possibly aspirational link to the Wiltshire nobility, has led many scholars to the conclusion that Vaughan had actually invented the bedwork method of irrigation (Taylor *et al* 2006). Some authorities have consequently claimed it was the success of these chalkland bedworks that induced farmers in other more hilly regions to adopt catch-meadow irrigation, implying catch meadows developed in the 17th century (Bettey 1999). Recent work has concluded that Vaughan's water meadows were in fact simply a variety of catch meadow, most likely established by his predecessor and simply extended by Vaughan (Taylor *et al* 2006, 44–6).

Functionally, Vaughan's writings indicate that his irrigation scheme was intended only to produce an enhanced hay harvest, not support livestock levels. A version of floating with objectives closer to that of Exmoor's catch meadows was certainly in use in some parts of the country by the early 16th century. John Fitzherbert's *Boke of Surveying and Improvement*, first published in 1523 states:

> yf there be any rynning water or lande flode that may be sette or brought to run ouer the meadows from the tyme that they be mowen vnto the beginning of May / and the will be much bettr and it shall kylle / drowne / and driue away the moldywarpes [moles] and fyll up the lowe places with sande & make the grounde euyn and good to mowe. All maner of waters be good / so that they stand nat styll vpon the gounde / But especially that water that cometh out of a towne from eury mannes mydding or don gehyll is best / and will make the medowes moost rankest. And fro the bgynning of May tyll ye medowes be mowen and the hay goten in / the waters wolde be set by and ron another way.
>
> (Fitzherbert 1523, quoted in Cook *et al* 2003, 158)

How much earlier catch meadows were adopted in the south-west is uncertain. Unlike bedworks, which were a much larger undertaking, it is likely that the creation of catch meadows was a task for individual farmers or tenants, with maintenance undertaken as part of their routine annual tasks. As such, their creation on Exmoor would generate little documentary evidence. Deserted medieval

Fig 3.8
A map of Halberton illustrates the importance of water management in early 17th-century Devon. [Courtesy of Devon County Record Office, © Devon County Council]

settlements on Exmoor have so far yielded no evidence of artificial irrigation schemes (Brown 2005; Riley and Wilson-North 2001). It is probable that catch meadows do have medieval antecedents, but where evidence does exist for medieval irrigation systems beyond Exmoor, it is in a monastic context (Cook et al 2003; Marshall 1796, 206–7).

Catch meadows outside the former royal forest are associated with some of Exmoor's earliest farmhouses, which date from the 16th or 17th centuries, and their creation may indeed be contemporary. However, the date of individual catch meadows is very difficult to ascertain. They are by their nature dynamic systems, which may have been cut and re-cut regularly, their plan changing with the needs of the farm. A catch meadow may have been altered, abandoned and completely replanned any number of times since the system was first used. The evidence we see today may represent only the last few times that the system was used (Taylor 2007, 32). Nevertheless, it is clear from aerial photographs that catch meadows are widespread throughout greater Exmoor and it is likely that they have been at the forefront of farm-scale reclamation since at least the 18th century.

Catch meadows: aims, construction and operation

On Exmoor and elsewhere, water meadows originated as part of mixed farming. Sheep or cows grazed the pasture of the catch meadow by day but were folded at night on the arable fields, providing an important source of fertiliser (Wade-Martins and Williamson 1994; Williamson 2000). The headage of livestock that a farm could sustain was thus directly linked to its productivity (Brown 2005). The aim of catch-meadow irrigation on Exmoor was therefore to maximise the livestock carrying capacity of a farm. This was achieved by improving the quality and quantity of feed available to the farmer at the least productive times of the year: the harsh months of winter and early spring. From October to April grass grows very little and livestock are completely dependant on the fodder provided by the farmer. The situation is most difficult in the months immediately before the new spring growth. The hardships that often arose in March and April, both for man and beast, have resulted in this time of year becoming known as the 'hungry gap'.

Catch meadows were created to relieve this pressure in two ways.

First, by regularly flushing the pasture with running water the temperature of the soil could be raised just enough to stimulate growth. This allowed livestock some winter grazing and, according to many 19th-century advocates, also had the beneficial effect of promoting the growth of more nutritious varieties of grass. Regular flushes, especially from 'warm' springs, also protected grass from frost damage during cold snaps. More importantly, water meadow irrigation encouraged an early spring growth, reducing the time that livestock was reliant on winter fodder by producing an 'early bite' and allowing lambs to be turned out several weeks if not months earlier than would otherwise have been possible. Winter irrigation often began in November and continued intermittently through until March, the slopes being watered in short bursts lasting from two to six days, depending on the farmer's preference (Roals 1845; Williamson and Cook 2003).

Second, catch meadows provided an additional hay crop. In early summer livestock could be moved from the water meadow onto fresh pasture, the grass grown and cut for winter fodder. By continuing to water the meadows, the extra moisture would stimulate and enhance the growth of grass, allowing a second or even third hay crop to be taken (Cutting and Cummings 1999, 164). It was the increase in hay that drove the Brendon farmer John Roals to create 12 hectares of catch meadow on his farm in the 1820s, an investment that repaid him with up to 0.5 ton of hay per hectare, an increase of at least 50 per cent (Roals 1845, 519). This aspect of the technology increased Robert Smith's enthusiasm for catch meadows, as he wrote in 1856:

> The subject of hillside catch-meadows in a rough and rugged climate abounding with valuable springs and a rainy climate cannot well be too forcibly dwelt upon, and the more so as I have mown full two tons of hay per acre from this class of meadow when properly improved, which some seven years past were worthless hillsides.
>
> (Smith 1856, 384)

For generations traditional catch meadow irrigation had enabled the Exmoor hill farmer to maximise the potential of his holding. Catch meadows were fundamental to the economic

Fig 3.9a and b
Despite their close proximity,
it is likely that each farm's
catch meadow developed
individually, using a
separate water source.
[(a) OS 72065 (V) 191;
(b) © John Hodgson]

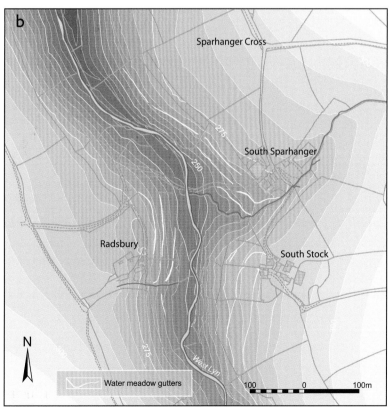

life of the farm, increasing crops and providing fat lambs for market. Although rarely mentioned in early documentary sources, they were so important that almost every farm on and around Exmoor had one, no matter how small or simple.

Almost every farm on and around Exmoor has some evidence for irrigation. Many catch meadows are relatively small and simple, consisting of three, four or five short gutters only a few hundred metres long, irrigating the infield directly below the farm.

Small catch meadows like this are found at South Stock, South Sparhanger and Radsbury farms to the south of Lynton and Lynmouth. Despite their close proximity, it is likely that each farm's catch meadow developed individually, using a separate water source.

Although surviving catch meadows are potentially ancient, the earthwork remains represent only the final phases of use. It is rare that evidence for longer periods of use can be read in the landscape (but *see* Fig 3.10).

Catch meadows are seen by many as the poor cousins of bedworks, often referred to as a less satisfactory, less intensive or less sophisticated

Fig 3.10
Wilway Farm, south-west of
Dulverton, where, from
above, the earthworks tell a
story of recutting and reuse
possibly stretching back
hundreds of years.
[RAF 39/3821 (V) 0202]

form of irrigation (Bettey 1999; Curtis 1971; Williamson and Cook 2003). Indeed, the principle of this technology is very simple. Water was diverted from a stream or spring along narrow water channels, known variously as main water-carriages, carriage gutters, carriers, headmains or more often simply called gutters, which ran along the contour of the hill or combe slope.

The carriers were made to overflow, the overspill irrigating the slopes in a moving sheet of water before returning to the stream, either directly or via another channel, often called a tail drain, below. Larger or more complex catch meadows may contain more than one main water-carriage gutter and any number of subsidiary gutters, but the essential principle remained unchanged.

By means of drains, sluices or weirs, water was conveyed to the meadow, along a main carriage gutter, or carrier, a channel nearly 1m wide and 15cm deep. The carriers were laid out carefully to ensure that the desired flow of water was achieved. In the mid-19th century a gradient of 1:396 was recommended for the 'main carriages' of Exmoor catch meadows (Smith 1851, 141).

Catch meadows with appropriately abundant water supplies often had more than one carrier, each tapping the water source in sequence as the system followed the fall of a combe. The carriers were often slightly embanked on their downslope side turning them into mini-reservoirs to collect a body of water sufficient to flood the field below.

At the desired time the waters were made to overflow. Each farmer might have a preferred method for doing this. Recorded techniques included designing the carrier to gradually narrow to a point, making small cuts through the downslope bank, or simply blocking it with turf dams or 'stops' at strategic points along its length (Taylor *et al* 2006). If a catch meadow crossed a number of fields, sluices or culverts could be built into fences to provide more control (Brown 2005). By these means a particular length of carrier could be made to overflow on command, spilling a controlled amount of water over a specific area of meadow, for a desired length of time. Once an area had been irrigated, the stops could be moved or new cuts made and old ones blocked, and the flooding of the next section of meadow could begin.

Between the main carriers, larger catch meadows usually contained extra, smaller gutters, up to 45cm wide and 13cm deep. Unlike carriers, however, these did not tap the water supply and were carefully engineered to be perfectly level. Arrayed in parallel lines below or between the main carriers, these gutters collected and evenly redistributed the thin sheet of water flowing from the carriers, preventing it from converging into small rivulets or gullies, important if irrigating irregular or unimproved ground. Every aspect of catch meadow construction was carefully considered to offer more control to the farmer (Smith 1851, 141).

Further refinements improved the flexibility and efficacy of Exmoor's catch meadows. A good water supply was essential, but was also often variable, finite or even shared with other farms, which could lead to disputes. On detached or remote catch meadows ponds could be dug adjacent to the carriers, allowing water to be stored for later use. These reserves could irrigate land that would otherwise not be flooded during the winter or improve the hay harvest by providing an extra flush during the dry summer months.

It was in systems integrated with the farmstead, however, that catch meadows reached their highest levels of complexity. Water was diverted to the farmstead and was used to power a water wheel which in turn drove farm machinery such as a thresher, shearing equipment and root choppers. Once used in these ways, the 'waste' water was then 'passed through the yards and under every office' of the farm, gathering both animal and human waste into valuable liquid fertiliser (Smith 1851, 144). Collected in a specially constructed pond or manure clamp within or adjacent to the farmyard, these enriched waters were washed onto the slopes of Exmoor's farms through the catch meadow systems.

The most basic catch meadows consist of only one, two or three short gutters irrigating a small area of infield below the farmstead. Nonetheless, their apparent simplicity often belies a high degree of sophistication and economy. Each catch meadow was unique, a bespoke creation for the particular circumstances of each farm. All relied on a good water supply, and its availability and quantity defined the form and extent of each catch meadow. The quality of the water was also critical. Warm springs were preferred, and spring waters flowing from boggy and unimproved hills were even considered 'dangerous agents and … appeared formidable enemies' to irrigation (Smith 1851, 140). River or stream waters were also commonly used. The watercourse was dammed at a point upstream of the farm with one or more parallel carriage gutters diverting the waters to feed the catch meadows. River waters were also seen to be of varying quality but irrigation even with second-rate river waters was considered superior to fertiliser (Acland and Sturge 1851). Where both springs and streams were available, catch meadows were designed to integrate both supplies, as at Emmet's Grange, Smith's Exmoor farm.

Where water suitable for irrigation was not immediately available, farmers could create main carriage gutters of extraordinary length to procure a supply to create a catch meadow. A

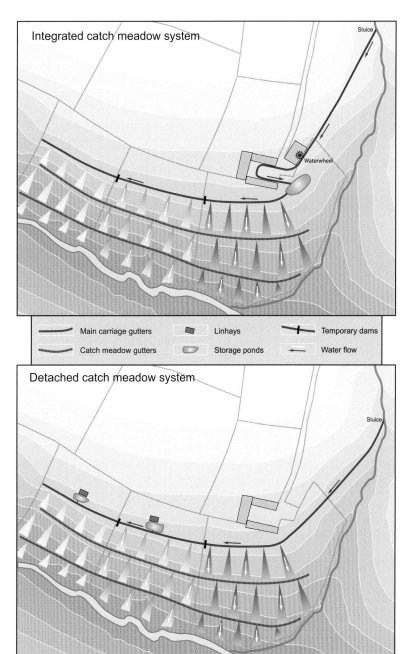

main carriage gutter, now abandoned, once carried spring water across Cheriton Ridge for over 2km, while another tapped a tributary of Badgworthy Water in Lank Combe, carrying its water supply for over 2.5km to irrigate the pasture of Cloud Farm. Such lengthy carriers may appear excessive, but could have performed a practical function. If no other waters were available, their great length would allow time in which the undesirable sediments could settle out from 'dangerous' peaty moorland waters.

Most Exmoor catch meadows were laid out on the infield or in-bye below the farmstead,

Fig 3.11
Schematic plan of catch meadow operation.
[© John Hodgson]

115

with gutters tapping a water supply higher than the farm (Brown 2005). This particular arrangement allowed the water to be passed through the farm and the water management was 'integrated' into the very structure of the farmstead buildings (Riley and Wilson-North 2001, 130; Taylor 2007, 29). By the 19th century, large estates as well as some individual farms, had further integrated water management into their farms as an important power source.

Other systems, like that at Cloud Farm, were unusual in running a catch-meadow headmain above the farmhouse. Catch meadows not integrated with farmsteads, such as that at Cloud Farm, have been termed 'detached' systems (Taylor 2007, 29). These worked on the same principle but were simpler in operation, only distributing what manure was transported to them (Brown 2005). This could be eased by the construction of open-fronted cattle sheds or linhays. When built above main carriage gutters these easily allowed manure to be mixed directly into the flowing waters of detached catch meadows, but the expense of construction ensured these were built only on the largest and most prestigious farms (Smith 1856, 355).

Unsurprisingly, after a suitable water supply, the most important factor in determining the layout of a catch meadow was the topography of the landscape to be irrigated. As Smith (1851, 141) stated, 'The arrangement of the "main water-carriages" depends solely on the formation of the land and supply of water.' The slopes of Exmoor's valleys and combes were steep, even for catch meadow irrigation, typically measuring between 10 and 18 degrees (Cook 1994). This incline was seen by Exmoor's 19th-century improvers, and perhaps earlier farmers, as advantageous as 'the same quantity of water will do much more work' (Smith 1851, 141).

In general, all 19th-century accounts seem to agree that the initial outlay was the greatest expense in creating a catch meadow. A long and involved process of preparation often accounted for much of these costs. On all but the steepest of Exmoor's slopes this typically involved a process known as paring and burning, which comprised removing, drying and burning the old turf. The ashes were then mixed into the soil by deep harrowing, which also levelled the ground with an eye to achieving an even flow of water over the surface. The ground could

Fig 3.12
Brightworthy Farm. The gutter system on the spur in the centre of the image is fed by a large rectangular pond (now dry) with sluice arrangement. The pond can be seen in the trees beside the farmyard.
[26884/002]

then be fertilised and cultivated with improving root crops such as turnips, which were eaten by sheep. The ground was then harrowed once again, levelled and rolled. Only then were carefully selected grasses planted. The final stage, that of making the gutters, occurred only after the sward had become well established, which could take anything from a few months to several years.

The cost of individual catch meadows appears to vary greatly. Roals' expenditure in converting 30 acres (12 hectares) of 'moory hill-side' to catch meadow came to over £5 an acre (Roals 1845). The creation of a meadow by the Reverend Jekyll, Rector of Withypool and Hawkridge, is described as costing 6s 3d per acre (Acland and Sturge 1851). At 12–15 shillings per acre, Robert Smith's catch meadows appear expensive, but still cheaper than the £2 per acre which seems to have been the average cost of a Devonshire water meadow (Smith 1851, 1856; White 1850). The outlay was seen as an acceptable price for the end result. Subsequent maintenance costs were low, the gutters only requiring to be recut or cleaned in the autumn in preparation for winter use (Riley and Wilson-North 2001).

Fig 3.13a and b
The long carriage gutter at Cloud Farm at Badgworthy Water.
[(a) Copyright and database right Crown Copyright and Landmark Information Group Ltd (All rights reserved 2014) Licence numbers 000394 and TP0024.
(b) RAF/106G/UK/1501 (RP) Frame 3352 13-May-1946 Lib 348]

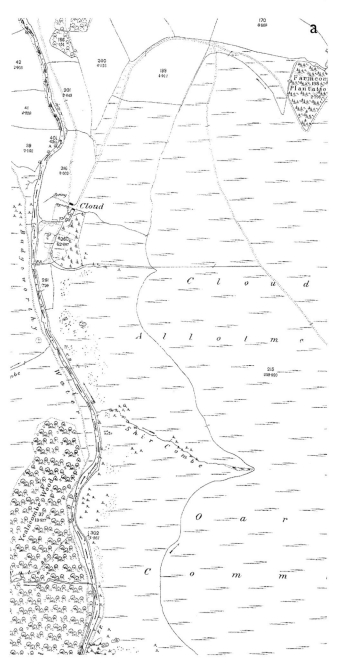

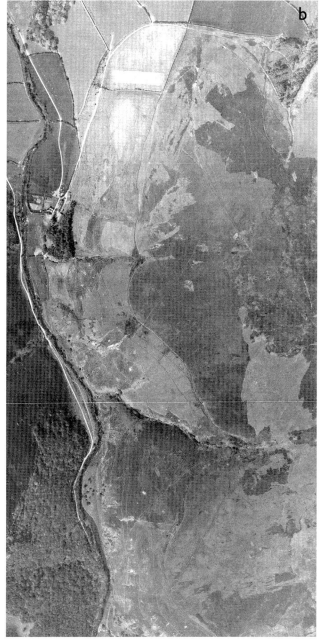

Fig 3.14
The Acland Hillside plough.
[Courtesy of Allerford
Museum]

Varying construction costs may in part reflect varying approaches to creating the catch meadow gutters. On gentle and thoroughly prepared slopes it is likely that many small landowners and farmers had sufficient knowledge to lay out their own gutters without the services of a specialist 'drowner', 'meadman' or 'gutterer'. For instance, Acland and Sturge (1851, 14–15) quote Jekyll describing how he laid out 3 hectares of catch meadow below his rectory at Tarr Steps. In contrast, the tenants of the Knight family's new farmsteads laid out

their catch meadows under the expert guidance of Robert Smith and the estate 'gutterer'. As Smith (1851, 141) states, the gutterer should be 'a man of some taste in the art of levelling, as the marking out the intermediate spaces upon irregular ground is found to be a nice point, that the water may flow in an even stream over the sides of the gutters'. The skill of the waterman or gutterer was well tested when setting out the water meadows of Exmoor, which boast some of the largest and most complex catch-meadow systems to be found anywhere in England.

The method used to cut catch-meadow gutters remains unclear, and may have varied from holding to holding or estate to estate. Acland and Sturge (1851, 15) conjectured that owing to his unusually low costs, Jekyll's account 'cannot be taken as including any spade labour'. This might imply that gutters were typically dug by hand. However, at Emmett's Grange on the Exmoor estate, Smith (1851, 142) describes how a common plough could be used to cheaply and easily cut the carriers and afterwards 'trimmed and levelled to the required form'. However, the ability of estates to influence specialisation and innovation is seen in the neighbouring Holnicote estate. Here

Fig 3.15
The catch meadow system
at West Harwood.
[26879/019]

Fig 3.16
Great Nurcott Farm catch
meadow.
[ENPA JAS 85042 078–9
29-AUG-1985]

Sir Thomas Dyke Acland was a keen agricultural improver who created the 'Acland Hillside' plough, a piece of equipment dedicated to the sole purpose of cutting catch meadow gutters.

In his 1851 treatise on the formation of catch meadows, Robert Smith states that for ease of watering, mowing, and the movement and shelter of livestock, the most convenient size for a water meadow is over 2 hectares in area. His recommendations were made perhaps based on observations of the many smaller and long-established catch meadows in the surrounding country.

In contrast, a small number of catch meadows associated with older Exmoor farms are significantly greater in size and complexity. For example, to the north of Winsford the integrated catch meadows of Great Nurcott Farm cover an area of nearly 16 hectares across both banks of the stream that supplies it with water.

An equally extensive but arguably more impressive catch meadow overlooks the River Avill from the slopes below the 17th-century West Harwood farmhouse. Also an integrated catch meadow, it formed part of a wider system of farm-scale water management, which incor-

porated an overshot water wheel, three or more supplementary ponds and a meadow-side linhay from which manure may have been added to the water supply. In total the catch meadow extends along the combe for over 1km and is composed of over 20 individual gutters crossing at least six fields. Each field is not much greater in area than Smith's ideal of around 2 hectares. However, unlike the model farms of the Exmoor estate, these large and complex catch meadows were imposed onto a landscape of existing fields, farms and former hamlets which was already ancient by the seventeenth century.

The remains of extensive catch meadows visible on aerial photographs represent only the final phase of a very long period of use. At both Great Nurcott and West Harwood farms, gutters have been re-cut or realigned and field boundaries removed, demonstrating that, unlike their 19th-century successors, such ancient water meadows were not imposed wholesale on the landscape but grew organically over time, adapting to the changing needs of the farm, yet still operating as part of a single large system.

Size, however, does not always equal complexity. A number of Exmoor's smaller water

Fig 3.17
As the combe slopes
approach the banks of the
River Barle, the gutters of
the catch meadow below
Knighton Farm become
much less regular in plan
to ensure maximum
irrigation of increasingly
uneven ground.
[RAF 30073 SFFO-0060 SS
8335/6 01-SEP-1952]

meadows appear simple but are in fact complex. In describing the Revd Joseph Jekyll's water meadows at Tarr Steps, Acland describes how 'One of the meadows in question is made on the steep hill side; the other on the bank of the river' and in his own account, Jekyll distinguishes between his *hill-side catch-meadows* and his *valley meadow* (Acland and Sturge 1851, 14). Nowhere on Exmoor have true valley bottom bedworks been recorded and, indeed, Exmoor's narrow and steeply incised combes are poorly suited to this method of irrigation. Jekyll's 'valley meadow' must therefore have been something else. From his own description, after

clearing, improving and cultivating the stony and scrubby field, Jekyll laid it to grass and in the third year 'conveyed over it the Barle water in a 2-feet gutter, through its centre, cutting the smaller gutters, some at right angles, some serpentine, from the main gutter according to the level' (Acland and Sturge 1851, 15).

This is not a bedwork or catch meadow, but rather describes a type somewhere between the two, a hybrid form of water meadow laid out on the slopes of gentler valley floors. Similar valley bottom catchworks have been identified elsewhere in lowland England (Cutting and Cummings 1999), but laying out gutters to

Fig 3.18
No improvable pasture was
wasted on the improved
farm. A paired system of
catch meadow and hybrid
water meadow irrigate the
land above the East Lyn
River, near Brendon village.
[NMR OS/95026 089–090
12-MAR-2007]

achieve good coverage over a narrow but gently inclined and irregular valley bottom would have been a difficult task, requiring the expert attention of the waterman or gutterer. Unfortunately no trace of Jekyll's valley bottom water meadow is now visible, but aerial survey has revealed that he was by no means unique in adopting this hybrid approach to irrigation. In fact, paired water meadows comprising both hillside catch meadows and valley floor sub-types may have been a well established, if less common, feature of traditional irrigation on Exmoor.

The infield of Knighton Farm in Withypool and Hawkridge was irrigated by a small spring-fed and possibly integrated catch meadow. Below this system, however, thicker and more irregular and sinuous gutters are arrayed. Using the same spring waters, these channels would have been skilfully cut to exploit the subtle undulations of the almost level valley floor to irrigate the bank of the River Barle, before flowing on to join the river.

To the east of Brendon village, the higher slopes above Leeford Lane are irrigated by a small detached catch meadow that taps a stream rising nearly 2km to the south on Tippacott Ridge. The catch meadow waters were probably enriched with manure from the appropriately named Waterlet Linhay, a cow shed adjacent to the source of the main carriage gutter. Below Leeford Lane, however, a narrow sliver of undulating combe bottom pasture on the southern bank of the East Lyn River was also considered valuable enough to be irrigated.

Case study
Emmett's Grange

Roughly 3km to the south-west of Simonsbath is Emmett's Grange. Built by 1844, it is the best surviving example of a planned farm on the Knight estate (Orwin and Sellick 1970, 78). From 1848 to 1865 the farm was tenanted by Robert Smith, the Knights' land agent, and became a showcase for his agriculturally progressive policies, a plan of the farm even featuring, albeit anonymously, in his prize-winning essay of 1856 on *Bringing Moorland into Cultivation*. The house itself is carefully sited and looks southwards down Kinsford Water. It has a somewhat grandiose front with an elaborate porch on its main façade and the lawn is separated from the fields by a ha-ha. There are plantations and shelter belts, linhays, ponds and gutters (some cut through rock outcrops) as well as stock handling facilities. The whole farm is a confident assertion of the value and potential of agricultural improvement at its peak in the mid-19th century.

The published plan also expresses Smith's confidence and illustrates many of the 'durable improvements', which, under Smith's management, the Exmoor estate encouraged their own tenants to develop. Many of the improvements that Smith depicts survive on the ground or have been recorded from aerial photographs, confirming that Smith's improving rhetoric was to some degree translated into reality. Extensive water-management features are among the most obvious characteristics depicted and it is notable that the 1856 plan makes no distinction between drainage and irrigation, illustrating how both were perceived as part of a single system of farm-scale management. However, the correspondence between plan and reality is not exact, probably representing the ongoing, experimental nature of Smith's work at Emmett's Grange.

Smith's plan perhaps also indicated his aspirations for the farm, some of which may never have come to fruition. His essay champions integrated farm-scale water management from drainage to catch-meadow irrigation, with a water wheel powering farmyard machinery. Many of the estate farms effectively employed water power but Emmett's Grange may not have been one of them; although a carrier does appear to take water to the farmstead, there is little evidence that it ever turned a water wheel (Burton 1989, 91).

Fig 3.19
Emmett's Grange, the farmhouse and ha-ha.
[© Rob Wilson-North]

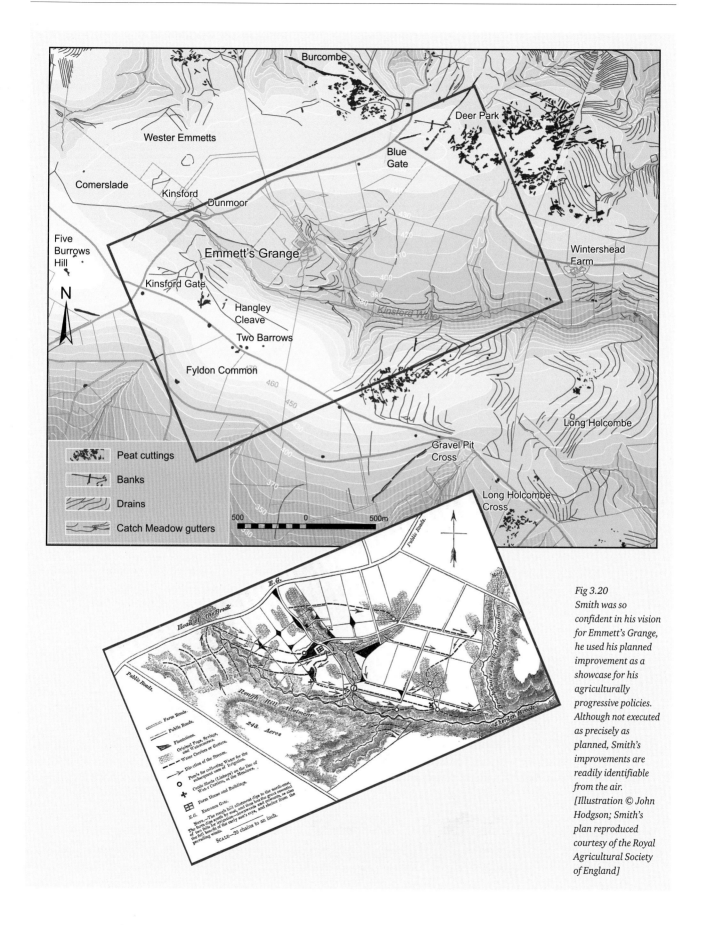

Peat cuttings

Banks

Drains

Catch Meadow gutters

500   0   500m

Burcombe

Deer Park

Blue Gate

Wester Emmetts

Comerslade

Kinsford
Dunmoor

Emmett's Grange

Wintershead Farm

Five Burrows Hill

N

Kinsford Gate

Hangley Cleave

Two Barrows

Kinsford Water

Fyldon Common

Long Holcombe

Gravel Pit Cross

Long Holcombe Cross

Fig 3.20
Smith was so confident in his vision for Emmett's Grange, he used his planned improvement as a showcase for his agriculturally progressive policies. Although not executed as precisely as planned, Smith's improvements are readily identifiable from the air.
[Illustration © John Hodgson; Smith's plan reproduced courtesy of the Royal Agricultural Society of England]

123

Here, in contrast to the regular gutters of the hillside catch meadow, the irregular and fan-like composition of the valley bottom gutters reflects the uneven surface of the meadow. The interconnecting cross-drains use the subtle slopes of the meadow to their advantage, to both irrigate and prevent water-logging before converging at the western end of the meadow below Longmeadow Linhay, and draining into the East Lyn River (Taylor *et al* 2006).

Disputes, interaction and etiquette

In many parts of the country a reliable water supply was a highly prized commodity. With the spread of floating as a method of irrigation using those same water supplies, conflicts were almost certain to arise. Disputes became commonplace between farmers and between farmers and others vying for the same resource, such as millers. From the 17th century, complex and binding legal agreements began to be drafted to clarify exactly who could use the water and at what times, from month to month and on what day of the week (Bettey 2007, 17; Cook *et al* 2003, 158).

By the early 19th century access to water for irrigation in East Devon was, at least sometimes, regulated by the drawing up of agreements between farmers which, for a small payment, agreed access to water supply and averted disputes during the vital months of the hungry gap. However, disagreements over water were still familiar in many parts of Devon and Somerset towards the end of the 19th century. For instance, by 1850 catch meadows were well established on the Killerton estate, the Devon seat of the agricultural improver Acland. However, so were quarrels over the catch meadow water supply shared by the neighbouring farms of Newhall and Francis Court (I Richardson, pers comm). A similar dispute arose between the miller and the local vicar when the clergyman wished to abstract water from the mill leat to irrigate his glebe lands (S Dymond, pers comm; DRO 1037M-0/E/3/3).

However, Exmoor is well provided with springs, streams and rivers, providing most farms with their own uncontested water supply for most months of the year. As such, and perhaps also because catch meadows were most intensively used in Exmoor's less densely populated upland areas, such conflicts rarely if ever arose on Exmoor, or if they did, they were resolved without recourse to the law!

Water-meadows, improvement and estates

The third class [of moorland farmland] consists of the flats and marshes in the valleys together with some portions of the adjacent hill-sides, which should be laid out for pasture and water-meadows. The practical bearing of such an occupation is that of stock-producing returns, consequently an eye must ever be had to this particular class of farming.
(Smith 1856, 355)

Smith's essay *Bringing Moorland into Cultivation* provides an indication of how water management was envisaged as one of the central strands of the reclamation of Exmoor in general, and the creation of a new moorland farm in particular.

Catch-meadow irrigation by the 18th century had already proved itself well suited to the narrow combes of Exmoor, and although it was not explicitly described as such, some degree of farm-scale water management was therefore established as part of traditional hill farming in the region. The practice of farm-scale water management and in particular catch meadow irrigation achieved its fullest expression on Exmoor at the hands of 19th-century estates and improvers.

Catch meadows were widely discussed among improvers and were, with the reclamation of moorland, one of the themes upon which Acland and Sturge reported to the Royal Agricultural Society of England in their discussion of the agriculture of Somerset in 1851.

By no means an entirely complimentary report, Acland and Sturge nonetheless highlighted Exmoor's catch meadows as one aspect of traditional farming worth preserving, and indeed expanding. Acland and Sturge also referred in very positive terms to the water meadows created by Robert Smith. Smith moved to Exmoor in 1848 to take up the post of Frederic Knight's land agent or steward, a post he held until 1865 (Orwin and Sellick 1970). Following his relocation from the more arid eastern counties of England, the efficacy of Exmoor's long-established catch meadows clearly had a profound effect on the farming practices of the already progressive Smith (1851, 140):

To see the Exmoor ewes with their early lambs (in January) feeding upon the verdant meadow, to me was a miracle; – first, the early period of lambing, and, secondly, the green meadow at such an inclement season.

However, it was not simply the improver's zeal that drove Smith's enthusiasm for catch meadows. The importance of catch meadows to reclamation and hill farming on Exmoor was at least in part a reflection of their monetary value. John Knight's early enthusiasm for water meadows was no doubt inspired in part by those he saw near Edinburgh in 1826, which commanded rent of £62 per acre (Orwin and Sellick 1970, 63). Nearly 20 years later Roals' 30 acres of Brendon Hill farmland increased in value from 2s an acre to 25s an acre following conversion to catch meadow. Robert Smith's fervour for irrigation was no doubt due in part to his recognition of the increased rent which could be charged for farmland incorporating such improvements.

However, first they needed to be built. Smith was able to translate his enthusiasm for catch meadows into reality by enshrining them as one of the 'durable improvements' provided for in the leases for the new Exmoor farms. Tenants would be compensated for the creation of catch meadows on the farm, among other improvements, both with low rents in the early years of their occupancy and reimbursement of costs of construction upon early ending of the tenancy (Smith 1851, 146; 1856, 367–9).

In this way Smith ensured water management lay at the heart of the developing Exmoor estate's planned farms, ensuring all new catch meadows were truly 'integrated' systems. He was able to write as early as 1851 that (1851, 146):

New meadows are being laid out upon nearly every farm, the desire being to unite the uses of the water-wheel with that of the meadow below the yards, which is universally arranged to receive the sewerage and water after it has passed the wheel.

Although the farms of the surrounding parishes may have been labour rich, the new Exmoor estate was not and water-wheel-powered labour-saving machinery was needed, freeing up the farm's horses for other important tasks. Water power was ingeniously harnessed to power machines to carry out many basic farmyard tasks. Once again Robert Smith neatly summarises their use in relation to his own tenancy at Emmett's Grange farm:

To the water-wheel we must look for the future economy of the labour at the yard. It will perform the thrashing, chaff-cutting, grinding, root-slicing, &c.; the stream may also be so arranged as to wash all roots, cleanse all offices, collect the sewage of the establishment, and finally convey the refuse to the adjacent meadow below the farmstead, and so on to the end of the farm or meadows.
(Smith 1856, 355)

Later, water power even drove mechanical sheep shearers on the estate steadings.

The adoption of water-powered mechanisation on Exmoor farms reflects two important themes. First, it mirrors the wider changes in farming that were taking place nationwide. These re-imagined both farming processes and the physical farmstead as part of an industrial process hungrily pursuing increased efficiency. This view characterised the 'high farming' of the mid- to late 19th century. It changed the shape of farms and farm buildings, perhaps most visible on Exmoor in the development of bank barns, a hill-farming innovation originating on Cumbrian estates but adopted throughout the west of England, and now fundamental to the character of Exmoor farmsteads (Wade Martins 2002). Although at the forefront of 19th-century farming technology, the integration of water power into Exmoor's farms also reflects the inherent pragmatism of Exmoor hill farming. Whereas by the mid-19th century farms in many other parts of the country were increasingly employing portable steam engines to replace horse power in many of the normal activities of the farmyard, the use of steam power never became established on Exmoor, no doubt due in part to the expense and difficulty of transporting fuel to isolated farms. Instead, estate-driven improvement led to increasingly innovative and efficient management of naturally occurring water power (Brown 2009, 42–3).

Water power was not seen as being in any way inferior to steam. Economic constraints meant that the new Exmoor farmsteads were simple and even severe in appearance. However, between 1858 and 1860 Smith was able to indulge his enthusiasm for farm-scale integrated water management without such financial constraints. In his design for the home farm complex at Eastwood Manor at East Harptree in Somerset, Smith took this technology to its logical conclusion. Behind architecturally elaborate limestone façades, an enormous 9m diameter waterwheel powered the fully automated machinery of what has been described as 'the ultimate application of factory design to a farm', a fully enclosed twin yard complex built using the latest building materials such as cast iron and corrugated iron to create a farm at the forefront of farming technology (Wade Martins 2002, 134). We can only imagine what Smith might have designed for Exmoor if resources had permitted and he had been encouraged in that particular direction.

Nonetheless, pragmatic water management was so fundamental to the efficient operation of Exmoor's new farms that it even influenced their plan. On the estate farms field boundaries or fences were not simply barriers, but were multi-functional components of the new designed farming landscape. First, while correctly placed fences would provide shelter, small diamond shaped or triangular plantations built into the intersections or corners of new fences would provide extra 'succour' for livestock, particularly important during the cold winter months when the sheep were grazing the new growth of the catch meadow (Smith 1851, 145; 1856, 362).

Second, and perhaps more significantly, new fences formed part of the farm's system of water management and irrigation. The ditches dug during the construction of cross-fences, those boundaries which subdivided the infields within a holding, and particularly those which divided hilltop from valley meadow, were put to use as conduits connecting distant parts of the holding, ensuring that all became integrated into one efficient and unified whole. In writing about his experiments at Emmett's Grange, Smith (1851, 146) explained:

This brings me to the importance of having all new fences (where practicable) laid out by the 'spirit level;' that, while some may be formed to collect the surface water from the upper lands to a certain point, most eligible for a pond, others may be arranged to convey the water from the pond to the nearest meadows. By this plan the 'water-carriages' are made when the 'sodfence' is erected, consequently included in its cost – a saving of at least a shilling per chain – the carriage formed in an otherwise useless dike and the land saved on which the dike would otherwise have been cut ... Water-carriage fences are now (where practicable) universally adopted upon this property.

In this way the requirements of farm-scale water management and irrigation defined the enclosed farming landscape of the former royal forest of Exmoor.

Conclusion

Hope Bourne in *Living on Exmoor* (1991) described the Knight family's attempts less as 'reclamation' but rather as a 'battle with the moor' in which they 'fought it for many years … but in the end they never really tamed the Forest. The gale-swept, bog-blanketed heights still remain as they ever were, a last stronghold of sullen nature defiant against man.'

It is tempting to see the Knight enterprise as a failure, but its mark on the Exmoor of today is a profound one. Most of the Knight farms continue to be in use and are still farming. Much of the land that was enclosed on the south-facing slopes of the Barle valley around Simonsbath is still productive farmland. The road network that John Knight built has transformed the pattern of communication across Exmoor and in a real sense has made the wilder moors less remote. Simonsbath, although still a tiny village, is very much in existence, although as a village at the heart of a thriving estate it is a failure. Families who were drawn to Exmoor as Knight tenants, have survived to this day. The moorland drains and peat cuttings are gradually silting up and disappearing, but from the air the scale of the enterprise can still be appreciated.

That is the lasting impact of the Knight family on Exmoor. But there is also the terrible loss of moorland. There is the destruction of prehistoric settlements, standing stones and other earlier remains, which no doubt existed across the farms at the centre of the former royal forest.

The Knight enterprise also contributed to the historic landscape itself. For, in effacing the evidence for earlier periods, the Victorian improvers made their own mark on the landscape and have added to the narrative in a way that they could not possibly have imagined. The 'archaeology of improvement' provides a rich legacy of historic buildings, industrial archaeology, technical innovation, folly and aspiration. It is as instructive today as the abandoned Bronze Age fields, which tell of unsustainable farming practice in the face of climate change nearly 3,000 years ago.

Outside the former royal forest, the evidence of farming practice on the commons and on individual farms during and since the medieval period has profoundly shaped the landscape in different ways. Individual pioneer farmers ploughed lonely furrows on the moor, leaving the corrugations that can still be traced on the surface; commoners and smallholders pooled their labour and together turned woodland and 'waste' into productive farmland, their efforts rewarded by individual fields whose shared curving pattern still betrays their communal origin.

Elsewhere the subtle outlines of abandoned peat workings still defy detailed understanding but nevertheless acknowledge the countless spring days of back-breaking labour by individual commoners to provide winter fuel for the farmhouse hearth.

This book has provided testimony – in the form of archaeological evidence – of the collaboration and innovation of individual farmers from the medieval period to present times. Their legacy is writ large in the landscape. Ultimately Exmoor's story is the struggle for survival. As one Exmoor hill farmer's wife explained, 'we have been clinging on here by our fingernails since the Knights built this farm'.

GLOSSARY

Aerial survey The recording of archaeological sites and landscapes from the air; it includes taking new photographs and interpretation and mapping from both new and archive photographs.

Agistment The grazing of waste within a royal forest or the money received for it.

Brown earths Non-alluvial loamy soils with a non-calcareous subsoil without significant clay enrichment (Thompson, D 2007).

Carriage gutter The principal water channel of a catch meadow. Also known as main water-carriages, carriers, headmains or simply gutters.

Catch meadow A type of hill or valleyside water meadow consisting of one or more water channels, known as gutters.

Common right of marl The common right to take sand and gravel.

Common rights, rights of common Rights which one or more persons may have to take or use some portion of that which another man's soil naturally produces. Established rights of common include pasture, piscary, turbary, marl, estovers and pannage.

Cropmarks Variations in vegetation growth revealing the presence of buried archaeology.

Drowner A term for a specialist in the construction and operation of water meadows. Also see *Waterman*.

Earthworks The upstanding remains of archaeological sites or landscape features.

Enclosure The act of constructing boundary fences, walls or ditches to divide previously unenclosed land into fields, or used to describe the enclosed area itself.

Estovers The common right to take wood for the commoner's house or holding, usually limited to smaller trees, bushes such as gorse and fallen branches.

Field gutter system A type of hill or valleyside water meadow consisting of one or more water channels, known as gutters.

Frith Small branches or twigs used to create 'dead-hedges' on top of temporary enclosures.

Gutter Narrow water channels arrayed in parallel lines below or between the main carriage gutters on catch meadows.

Gutterer An expert in the creation of water meadows. Also often known as a 'drowner' or a 'meadman'.

Inclosure The legal term used to describe the process of the consolidation or extension of private landownership over land previously held in common. *or* The legal process of enclosure, often by Act of Parliament, whereby lands previously held in common were divided up into private ownership. Inclosure usually resulted in the loss of common rights.

Levancy and couchancy From the French *levant et couchant*. This is the rule under which the number of animals that could be pastured on a common was limited by the requirement that they must be maintained in winter on the land to which the rights were attached. Literally, the animals that can "get up and lie down" on the land to which the right is attached.

LiDAR Light detection and ranging. A remote sensing technique commonly employing airborne laser scanning to create Digital Terrain Models (English Heritage 2010).

Mast or pannage The common right to turn out pigs for a period in autumn to eat mast (acorns and other nuts).

NMP/National Mapping Programme An English Heritage programme with the aim of enhancing the understanding of past human settlement by providing primary information and synthesis for all archaeological sites and landscapes visible on aerial photographs or other airborne remote sensed data.

Oblique aerial photographs Aerial photographs taken at an 'oblique' angle, usually from the window of a high-winged light aircraft. Oblique photographs are frequently taken specifically for archaeological purposes.

Parchmarks A type of cropmark caused by the inhibited growth of vegetation over buried archaeological features such as masonry in dry conditions.

Paring and burning A traditional form of land management, carried out for thousands of years, whereby sections of moor are burnt in controlled fires to encourage regeneration of moorland vegetation for wildlife and grazing.

Pasture The common right to pasture cattle, horses, sheep or other animals on the common land. The most widespread common right.

Perambulation A traditional means of defining the legal extent of area by walking around it, often annually; also known as 'beating the bounds'.

Piscary The common right to fish.

Podzolisation A soil forming process that occurs in humid conditions particularly where coniferous and acidic vegetation dominates. Organic material leaches from the upper layers and is deposited in lower layers, creating distinct, ash-grey horizons.

Soilmarks Variations in soil colour or tone, usually visible from the air, revealing the fill of archaeological features brought to the surface by ploughing.

Stagnohumic gley Mainly upland soils intermediate between stagnogleys and peats with a humose or peaty topsoil (Thompson, D 2007).

Stagnopodzols Mainly upland soils with a peaty topsoil and/or a periodically wet, faintly mottled bleached subsurface horizon, overlying an iron-enriched layer (Thompson, D 2007).

Stinting Limitations on the number of animals and how long they could be pastured on a common, intended to prevent abuses of the resources of the common and conflict between commoners.

Telling From the Old English *tellan*, meaning to count or take account.

Telling house A structure where shepherds gathered to count the sheep as they were moved from the moor at the end of the pasturing season.

Turbary The common right to take sods of turf (peat) for fuel.

Vertical aerial photographs Aerial photographs taken looking directly (vertically) down, giving the observer a map-like view of a landscape at a uniform scale. They are rarely taken for archaeological purposes.

Water meadow Areas of grassland irrigated by diverting water from a neighbouring river or stream to produce a rich hay crop and more abundant grazing.

Waterman A term for a specialist in the construction and operation of water meadows. Also see *Drowner*.

PRIMARY SOURCES

Devon Record Office, Letter of 20 May 1769 from Sir T D Acland to James Willie of Steer's Cottage, Horner (DRO 1148 M add 2/67)

Devon Record Office, Correspondence of 24 August 1772 (DRO 1148 M add 2/67)

Devon Record Office, 1788 The Holnicote land agent's accounts list (DRO 1148 M add. Agents Accounts Cridland)

Devon Record Office, Betty Elsworthy application for a plot to grow potatoes on land in Allerford (DRO 1148 M add 21/E1)

Devon Record Office, May Taylor of Dunster (DRO 1148 M add 21/E1)

Devon Record Office, 1769 James Willie application to enclose a patch on Horner Hill (DRO 1148M add 2/67)

Devon Record Office, Enclosure of Lyn Down, 1860 (DRO inclosure map 54)

Devon Record Office, Enclosure of Kentisbury Down (DRO inclosure map 49)

Devon Record Office, Court Rolls Manor of Stoke Fleming 1467–1468 (DRO 902M/M22)

Devon Record Office, Map of Halberton (DRO 6065Z)

Devon Record Office, Dispute between the miller and the local vicar (DRO 1037M-0/E/3/3)

Somerset Record Office, 18th-century survey of Higher Blackland farm near Withypool DD/SF 3147

BIBLIOGRAPHY

Acland, T D and Sturge, W 1851 'The farming of Somersetshire'. *Journal of the Royal Agricultural Society of England* **11** (2)

Aston, M 1983 'Deserted farms on Exmoor and the lay subsidy of 1327 in West Somerset'. *Proceedings of the Somerset Archaeology and Natural History Society* **127**, 71–104

Aston, M 1999 'Medieval rural settlement', *in* Webster, C J (ed) *Somerset Archaeology: Papers to Mark 150 Years of the Somerset Archaeological and Natural History Society.* Taunton: Somerset County Council, 93–98

Barber, M 2011 *A History of Aerial Photography and Archaeology: Mata Hari's Glass Eye and other stories.* Swindon: English Heritage

Barnes, W 1888 *Poems of Rural Life in the Dorset Dialect.* London: Kegan Paul, Trench, Trubner

Barrett, N 2004 'The Pinkery Canal Exmoor, Somerset', English Heritage Unpublished Report, Archaeological Investigations Report Series A/07/2004

Barron, J 1903 *The Northern Highlands in the Nineteenth Century: Newspaper Index and Annals.* Volume 1, 1800–1824

Beaumont, M 1989 'Tithes and enclosures', *in* Combe Martin Local History Group, *Out of the World and into Combe Martin.* Combe Martin, Devon: Combe Martin Local History Group

Beeton, I 1861 *Mrs Beeton's Book of Household Management.* London: S.O. Beeton

Berry, N 2003 'Archaeological and historic landscape survey of West Lyn Farm, Lynton, Devon'. Unpublished Report for the National Trust

Bettey, J 1999 'The development of water meadows in the southern counties', *in* Cook, H and Williamson T (eds) *Water Management in the English Landscape.* Edinburgh: Edinburgh University Press

Bettey, J 2007 'The floated water meadows of Wessex: a triumph of English agriculture', *in* Cook, H and Williamson, T (eds) *Water Meadows, History, Ecology and Conservation.* Cambridge: Windgather Press

Billingsley, J 1794 *A General View of the Agriculture of Somerset: With Observations on the Means of its Improvement.* Board of Agriculture, London: W Smith

Blake, W J 1915 'Hooker's synopsis chorographical of Devonshire'. *Transactions of the Devonshire Association* **47**, 334–348

Bourne, H L 1991 *Living on Exmoor.* Wellington: Exmoor Books

Bowden, M, Brown, G and Smith, N 2009 *An Archaeology of Town Commons in England; 'A very fair field indeed'.* London: English Heritage

Brooks, H 1992 'North Thorne excavation'. Unpublished North Devon Archaeological Society Report

Brown, G 2005 'Irrigation of water meadows in England', *Ruralia* **V**, 84–92

Brown, J 2009 *Steam on the Farm, A History of Agricultural Steam Engines 1800 to 1950.* Ramsbury: Crowood Press

Burton, J 2002 'The Cistercian adventure', *in* Robinson, D (ed.) *The Cistercian Abbeys of Britain; Far from the Concourse of Men.* London: English Heritage

Burton, R A 1989 *The Heritage of Exmoor.* Privately published

Burton, S H 1969 *Exmoor.* London: Hodder & Stoughton

Camden, C 1610 *Britain, or, a Chorographicall Description of the most flourishing Kingdomes, England, Scotland, and Ireland* London: George Bishop and John Norton (digital version accessed at http://www.visionofbritain.org.uk/travellers/Camden)

Chanter, J F 1907 'Swainmote courts of Exmoor, and the Devonshire portion and purlieus of the forest'. *Transactions of the Devonshire Association* **39**, 267–301

Clayden, P 2003 *Our Common Land: The Law and History of Common Land and Village Greens*, 5th edn. Henley-on-Thames: Open Spaces Society

Cook, H 1994 'Field scale water-management in Southern England to AD 1900'. *Landscape History* **19**, 53–66

Cook, H and Williamson, T (eds) 1999 *Water Management in the English Landscape.* Edinburgh: Edinburgh University Press

Cook, H and Williamson, T (eds) 2007 *Water Meadows. History, Ecology and Conservation.* Cambridge: Windgather Press

Cook, H, Stearne, K and Williamson, T 2003 'The origins of water meadows in England'. *Agricultural History Review* **51**(2), 155–162

Curtis, L F 1971 *Soils of Exmoor Forest.* Soil Survey Special Survey No. 5. Whitstable: Harpenden

Cutting, R and Cummings, I 1999 'Water meadows: their form, operation and plant ecology', *in* Cook, H and Williamson, T (eds) *Water Management in the English Landscape.* Edinburgh: Edinburgh University Press

Defoe, D 1927 *A Tour Thro' the Whole Island of Great Britain, Divided into Circuits or Journies.* London: JM Dent and Co

Edmonds, E A, Mckeown, M C and Williams, M 1975 *British Regional Geology: South-west England.* London: HMSO

Eardley-Wilmot, H 1990 *Yesterday's Exmoor.* Dulverton: Exmoor Books

Edwards, R A 2000 *Exmoor Geology; Exploring the Landscapes, Rocks and Mines of the National Park.* Tiverton: Exmoor Books

English Heritage 2010 *The Light Fantastic: Using airborne lidar in archaeological survey.* Swindon: English Heritage

Everitt, A 2000 'Common land', *in* Thirsk, J (ed) *The English Rural Landscape.* Oxford: Oxford University Press, 210–35

Fairbairn, J 1823 *A treatise upon breeding, rearing, and feeding Cheviot and Black-faced sheep in high districts: With some account of – and a complete cure for, that fatal malady the rot: Together with observations on laying out and conducting a store farm.* Berwick-upon-Tweed: Printed for the author by W Lochhead, High-Street, 1823

Finberg, H P R 1971 'Ayshford and Boehill'. *Transactions of the Devonshire Association* **103**, 19–24

Findlay, D C, Colborne, G J N, Cope, D W, Harrod, T R, Hogan, D V and Staines, S J 1984 *Soils and Their Use in South West England.* Soil Survey of England and Wales Bulletin No. 4. Whitstable: Harpenden

Fox, H S A 1983 'Contraction: desertion and dwindling of dispersed settlement in a Devon Parish'. *Annual Report of the Medieval Village Research Group*, 31, 40–42

Francis, P 1984 'Catch meadow irrigation systems on Exmoor'. Unpublished BA dissertation

Fyfe, R 2011 'The pattern of vegetation development on Exmoor'. *Proceedings of the Somerset Archaeology and Natural History Society* **154**, 11–22

Fyfe, R, Brown, A and Rippon, S 2003 'Mid- to late-Holocene vegetation history of Greater Exmoor, UK: estimating the spatial extent of human-induced vegetation change'. *Vegetation History and Archaeobotany* **12**, 215–232

Garrett, C 2004 'An Enviable Possession: the Somerset Seat of the Knight Family. A report examining the possible existence and appearance of a nineteenth century designed landscape in and around Simonsbath, Exmoor'. Unpublished report for Exmoor National Park Authority

Gillard, M 2002 'The medieval landscape of the Exmoor region: enclosure and settlement in an upland fringe'. Unpublished PhD thesis, University of Exeter

Gillings, M, Pollard, J and Taylor, J 2010 'The Miniliths of Exmoor'. *Proceedings of the Prehistoric Society* **76**, 297–318

Gregory, J 2008 'Marginal environments and the idea of improvement: Transforming heathland and moorland landscapes c.1650–1850'. Unpublished PhD thesis, University of East Anglia

Hall, D 1981 'The origins of open field agriculture – the archaeological fieldwork evidence', *in* Rowley, T (ed) *The Origins of Open Field Agriculture.* London: Croom Helm, 22–38

Hallam, O 1978 'Vegetation and land use on Exmoor'. *Proceedings of the Somerset Archaeology and Natural History Society* **122**, 37–51

Hardin, G 1968 'The tragedy of the commons'. *Science* **162**(3859), 1243–1248

Hegarty, C and Toms, K 2009 'National mapping programme acceleration Exmoor National Park NMP; management and summary report'. Unpublished Report for English Heritage

Herring, P, Sharpe, A, Smith, J R and Giles, C 2008 *Bodmin Moor, An Archaeological Survey, Volume 2: The Industrial and Post-Medieval Landscape.* London: English Heritage

Holtom, J 2008 'Exmoor Commons'. *Exmoor Review* **49**, 52–55

Hooke, D 1989 'Pre-conquest woodland: its distribution and usage', *Agricultural History Review* **37**, 113–129

Horne, P 2011 'The English Heritage National Mapping Programme', *in* Cowley D C (ed) *Remote Sensing for Archaeological Heritage Management*, EAC Occasional paper No 5, EAC: Brussels, 143–151

Hoskins, W G 1954 *Devon.* London: Collins

Hoskins, W G and Dudley Stamp L 1963 *The Common Lands of England and Wales.* London: Collins

Hurst, D G and Wilson, D 1962 'Medieval Britain in 1961'. *Medieval Archaeology: Journal of the Society for Medieval Archaeology* **6–7**, 306–349

Jamieson, E 2001 'Larkbarrow Farm, Exmoor, Somerset; an archaeological survey by English Heritage'. Unpublished survey report

Jamieson, E 2003 'Archaeological survey work at Larkbarrow Farm'. *Proceedings of the Somerset Archaeology and Natural History Society* **146**, 17–26

Kerridge, E 1973 *The Farmers of Old England.* Sydney: Allen and Unwin

Land, W *Diaries of Mr Land, Hillway, Withypool, Somerset, 1913–1940.* Unpublished manuscript, ENPA HER

Letts, J 1991 'Thatch excavation record, Holnicote estate'. Unpublished report, National Trust

Lord Hailsham of St Marylebone 1991 *Halsbury's Laws of England*, 4th edn reissue, Vol 6. London: Butterworths

MacDermot, E T 1973 *The History of the Forest of Exmoor*, 3rd edn. Newton Abbot: David and Charles. (First published 1911)

Maltby, E 1995 'Soil development and ecological change on Exmoor', *in* Binding, H (ed) *The Changing Face of Exmoor.* Bristol: Exmoor Books, 33–42

Manwood 1615 *A Treatise and Discourse of the Lawes of the Forrest.* London: Printed for the Societie of Stationers

Marshall, W 1796 *Rural economy of the west of England: including Devonshire; and parts of Somersetshire, Dorsetshire, and Cornwell. Together with minutes in practice* (Volume 1)

Mold, E 1992 *Lynton and its Coast, a Brief History.* Barnstaple: Green Apple Publishing

Orwin, C S and Sellick, R J 1970 *The Reclamation of Exmoor Forest*, 2nd edn. Newton Abbot: David and Charles. (First published 1929)

Overton, M 1996 *Agricultural Revolution in England: The Transformation of the Agrarian Economy 1500–1850.* Cambridge: Cambridge University Press

Rackham, O 1998 *The History of the Countryside.* London: Phoenix

Ramsay, D 2009 *Unforgotten Exmoor: Volume One: Words and Pictures from a Vanished Era.* Dorchester: Rare Books and Berry

RCHME 1960 *A Matter of Time: An Archaeological Survey of the River Gravels of England Prepared by the Royal Commission on Historical Monuments (England).* London: HMSO

Riley, H 2013 'Hoaroak Valley: Historic landscape survey and analysis', 34. Report for Exmoor National Park Authority

Riley, H and Wilson-North, R 2001 *The Field Archaeology of Exmoor.* London: English Heritage

Rippon, S J, Fyfe, R M and Brown, A G 2006 'Beyond villages and open fields: the origins and development of a historic landscape characterised by dispersed settlement in South West England'. *Medieval Archaeology* **50**, 31–70

Roals, J 1845 'On converting a Moory hill-side into Catch Meadow'. *Journal of the Royal Agricultural Society of England* **6**, 518–521

Roberts, C G 1879 'Sutherland reclamation'. *Journal of the Royal Agricultural Society of England* **15** (2nd series), 397–487

Rose, F and Wolseley, P 1984 'Nettlecombe Park – its history and its epiphytic lichens: an attempt at correlation'. *Field Studies* **6**, 117–148

Rotherham, I D 2009 *Peat and Peat Cutting*. Oxford: Shire Publications

Sidney, S 1878 'Exmoor reclamation'. *Journal of the Royal Agricultural Society of England* **14** (2nd series), 72–97

Siraut, M 2009 *Exmoor: The Making of an English Upland*. England's Past for Everyone. Chichester: Phillimore & Co Ltd

Smart, C 2002 'A study of the relict field system on Winsford Hill, Exmoor'. Unpublished report, University of Exeter

Smith, R 1851 'Some account of the formation of hill-side catch-meadows on Exmoor'. *Journal of the Royal Agricultural Society of England* **12**, 139–148

Smith, R 1856 'Bringing Moorland into cultivation'. *Journal of the Royal Agricultural Society of England* **17**, 349–394

Stephens, H 1854 *The Book of the Farm; Detailing the Labours of the Farmer, Farm-Steward, Ploughman, Shepherd, Hedger, Cattle-Man, Field-Worker, and Dairymaid*. Edinburgh: William Blackwood

Straw, A 1995 'Aspects of the geomorphology of Exmoor', *in* Binding, H (ed) *The Changing Face of Exmoor*. Bristol: Exmoor Books, 13–25

Tarlow, S 2007 *The Archaeology of Improvement in Britain, 1750–1850*. Cambridge: Cambridge University Press

Taylor, C 2007 'The archaeology of water meadows', *in* Cook, H and Williamson, T (eds) *Water Meadows, History, Ecology and Conservation*. Oxford: Windgather Press

Taylor, C, Smith, N and Brown, G 2006 'Rowland Vaughan and the origins of downward floated water-meadows: a contribution to the debate'. *Landscape History* **28**, 35–51

Thompson, D 2007 *The National Soil Map and Soil Classification*. National Soil Resources Institute: Information paper. Cranfield University. http://www.landis.org.uk/downloads/Soil_classification.pdf (published online)

Tindley, A 2009 'The Iron Duke': land reclamation and public relations in Sutherland, 1868–95'. *Historical Research* **82**(216), 303–319

Turner, S 2007 *Ancient Countryside: The Historic Character of Rural Devon*. Devon Archaeological Society Occasional Paper 20

Vancouver, C 1808 *A General View of the Agriculture of Devon: With Observations on the Means of its Improvement. Drawn up for the Consideration of the Board of Agriculture and Internal Improvement*. London: Richard Phillips

Wade Martins, S 2002 *The English Model Farm, Building the Agricultural Ideal, 1700–1914*. Oxford: Windgather Press

Wade Martins, S and Williamson, T 1994 Understanding enclosure'. *Agricultural History Review* **42**, 20–37

Wade Martins, S and Williamson, T 1999 'Inappropriate technology? The history of "floating" in the North and East of England', *in* Cook, H and Williamson, T (eds) *Water Management in the English Landscape*. Edinburgh: Edinburgh University Press

White, W 1850 *History, Gazetteer and Directory of Devonshire*. London: Simpkin, Marshall

Williamson, T 2000 'Understanding enclosure'. *Landscapes* **1**(1), 56–70

Williamson, T 2002 *The Transformation of Rural England: Farming and the Landscape 1700–1876*. Exeter: University of Exeter Press

Williamson, T 2007 *Rabbits, Warrens & Archaeology*. Stroud: Tempus Publishing

Williamson, T and Cook, H 2003 'Introducing water meadows', *in* Cook, H and Williamson, T (eds) *Water Meadows, History, Ecology and Conservation*. Cambridge: Windgather Press

Winchester, A J L 1984 'Peat storage huts in Eskdale'. *Transactions of the Cumberland & Westmorland Antiquarian & Archaeological Society* **84** (new series), 103–115

Winchester, A J L 2000 'Dividing lines in a moorland landscape: territorial boundaries in Upland England'. *Landscapes* **1**(2), 16–32

Winchester, A J L 2004 'Moorland forests of medieval England', *in* Whyte, D and Winchester, A J L (eds) *Society, Landscape and Environment in Upland Britain*. Society for Landscape Studies Supplementary Series **2**, 21–56

Winchester, A J L 2006 'Common land in Upland Britain: tragic unsustainability or utopian community resource?', *in* Bosbach, F, Engels, J I and Watson, F (eds) *Umwelt und Geschichte in Deutchland und Grossbritannien – Environment and History in Britain and Germany* (Prinz-Albert-Studien Band 24). Munich

Winter, J 1999 *Secure from Rash Assault, Sustaining the Victorian Environment*. Berkeley: University of California Press

Youatt, W 1837 *Sheep: Their Breeds, Management, and Diseases. to Which is Added the Mountain Shepherd's Manual*. London: Baldwin and Cradock

Youell, R F 1974 'New evidence to explain the mystery of Pinkery Pond'. *Exmoor Review* **15**, 102–103

INDEX